Is there intelligent life on earth?

Is there intelligent life on earth?

By

Jack Catran

LIDIRAVEN BOOKS

Copyright © 1980 by Jack Catran
All rights reserved. This book, or parts thereof, must not be reproduced in any form without written permission from the publisher.

Library of Congress Catalog Card Number 80-80016
ISBN: 0-936162-29-5

First Printing September 1980
Printed in the United States of America

Second printing January 1981

Lidiraven Books
Box 5567, Sherman Oaks, CA 91413

For
Joseph and Rachel
who gave me life

And for all the
Heshies and Sadies
in America,
whose sharp tongues and
infallible noses for flim-flam
provided the shaping

Contents

Acknowledgements

One of the points made in this book is that none of us should be blamed or credited for our behavior; we are all products of our genetic inheritance, our past conditioning, and the current controls of our present environment. In a related sense, the book also emphasizes that there is no such thing as originality or creativity; we humans are all hit-or-miss dabblers aimlessly wandering in a strange world, and persistently working with a borrowed palette of ideas and values. If that is correct, then I cannot be faulted or credited for the thoughts expressed in these pages, since they were all helplessly assimilated during my years of contact with a multitude of competent people in the world of science; a contact made mostly through their writings, but sometimes through a personal involvement with the body of their work. If credit or blame *must* be assigned, then I am forced to point behind me to those who have motivated my bias, such as Jacque Fresco, Howard Scott, Wilton Ivie, B.F. Skinner, Charles Darwin, Albert Einstein, Jacques Loeb, Alfred Korzybski, and Ivan Pavlov. Surely they too, if challenged, would also point back to the works of other giants on whose shoulders they stood.

Introduction

There has been little public criticism of the "intelligent life on other planets" idea. As a result, enterprising scientists are having a field day appearing on television and in the popular press promoting their books on that subject to an uninformed public.

And it's more than promotion: a gold anodized aluminum plate is at this moment riding aboard *Pioneer 10* heading out into space. Scratched on the plate, which will take about 80,000 years just to arrive at our nearest star, is a "message" to other intelligent beings

Another example: There is a serious proposal drafted by scientists and engineers called Project Cyclops, which will cost about 10 billion dollars merely to cover its operation for the first 10 years. The Cyclops system will consist of twenty-five hundred giant antennae capable of two-way radio transmission to distant galaxies in order to "communicate" with intelligent civilizations.

Major American newspapers and magazines are whipping up a popular interest in the possibility of communicating with extraterrestrial civilizations. First there was a trickle. Now there is a steady stream. And, as we might expect, motion picture producers are profitably exploiting a public eager to stand patiently in long lines to be admitted to the latest flying saucer epic.

This book has two purposes: First, to reveal to the reader the outdated and erroneous ideas of our extraterrestrial believers, by presenting the modern, behavioral, definitions of *intelligence* and *man*.

1

Second, to point out how the power of science and technology to cure our social ills is being frustrated by the free enterprise system, which has as little relevancy to a science of production and distribution as ancient witchcraft has to modern medicine.

To repeat, there are two main themes: First, *Outer Space*, which points up what we believe are the flaws in the reasoning of our "intelligent-life-in-space" scientists. Second: *Planet Earth*, which details where the priorities of science *should be*, and describes how science and technology can solve our major problems right here on earth.

The scientist of today is caught in a conflict between two value systems: 1. The orderly world of science; 2. The non-scientific culture and language which nurtured him, shaped him, and continually controls him. It is difficult for us to grasp the full import of science because of the limits forced upon us by our social environment; at the same time, the forward march of technical progress, unidirectional and irreversible, steadily acts upon us without let-up.

In the pages ahead we attempt to identify the forces that are shaping our future; in which socially integrated computers will determine the most favorable decisions in the conduct of human affairs, where machines more than human will elevate government to the highest levels of efficiency, where millions of electronic slaves will control the production and distribution of goods and services and serve mankind in medicine and agriculture.

This is not the world of tomorrow of the science fiction writer. It is a look at the world as it is being shaped *today*, a world that will focus on the well-being of each individual, a world that is inevitable, barring catastrophic war.

If in the pages to follow we seem unduly harsh in our criticism of living scientists and others of eminence, they should understand at the outset that no disrespect is intended. And rather than play hob with the language, our expository style assumes that the many feminists who might object to the repeated use of the exemplary masculine singular and the construction "everybody (and) his", will perceive that it is meant to be generic, not gendered.

We do not expect that the first theme, *Outer Space*, will be enthusiastically received by the many Star Warriors, Third Kind Encounterers, flying saucer addicts, science fictioneers, and cereal box spacemen in our midst. Because the second theme, *Planet Earth*, points out why we think economists, sociologists, and politicians are unqualified to solve our complex social problems, it too might evoke a negative reaction from those who still haven't defected from the Old Order to the side of science.

The space exploration program to which we are presently committed is based on reality. There is no logical argument against its ultimate value. There may, of course, be "life" in space, but the "intelligent being" concept is based on an erroneous hypothesis. There are much grander and more awesome phenomena taking place in the universe, and soon the colonization of space will be a reality. Meanwhile, those billions of "communication" dollars proposed would better serve us if they were utilized by a board of science and technology as a down payment on a massive program to redesign America — a social design operated by scientists and engineers, attuned to the needs of *our* culture, not some mythical distant civilization's. If we could make a start in such a direction then, and only then, can we say that there is intelligent life on *Earth*.

Jack Catran
Los Angeles, California 1980

Before We Begin

The future is clear: jobs, wages, and money have been phased out; nothing has a price tag; personal possessions are no longer needed. Nationalism has been outdated and international disarmament is an established fact. Educational technology has made schools and teachers obsolete and the children are self-sufficient at age six. Busses, cars, and trains are a thing of the past. What do people do all day? They pursue culture, the arts, education, and each other, in an open and free society. Why do we bring all this up now? To make you salivate at the idea, to make you read the book beyond the first two chapters, and to make you say, "What a great notion. Where do I sign?"

From this point on, for the sake
of brevity, the "intelligent-life-
in-space" scientists shall be
referred to as the phILOSophers,
the ILOS representing Intelligent
Life in Outer Space.

1   Trap Thinking

*The question of "intelligent" life on other planets is almost
as old as the earth itself. In the 4th century B.C., the Greeks
founded a school of philosophy called Hylozoism, which
claimed that life existed all over the universe. And
Anaxagora's idea, Panspermia, which asserted that the
ethereal embios of life was omnipresent in the universe, is
equally as old. Early Christian phILOSophers, including
St. Augustine, shared the same point of view. Because the
mood of the times was geocentric, the views expressed by
Giordano Bruno in the 16th century, and all those before him,
were regarded as heresy by the then all-powerful clergy.*

*As the idea that the Earth was only one of many planets
spread, the belief in space aliens lost its one-time aura of
exclusiveness and became quite "trendy". Then, in 1877,
Schiaparelli discovered the "canals" of Mars, which gave the
idea an even bigger boost. Percival Lowell, an American
scientist, said that the canals were evidence of intelligent
beings, which led to the popular notion that Mars was
inhabited by people. In recent years, studies of the Moon and
the other planets by space scientists have cooled the zeal of the
phILOSophers. After Mars was found to be organism-free,
their optimism quickly faded and was replaced by a discreet
silence, later followed by a dampened enthusiasm, but not
hopelessness.*

Man has suffered a number of major blows to his
ethnocentric pride. First by Copernicus, who demonstrated

5

that the earth was not the center of the universe (the phILOSophers are still thinking in Earth terms). Second by Darwin, who stated that man is related to, and not something special or separate from, the other forms that inhabit the earth. Another blow was dealt by Freud, who maintained deterministically that man's behavior is not of his own choosing. And recently by B.F. Skinner and the radical behaviorists who, through the experimental analysis of behavior, have abolished "autonomous and intelligent" man and have shifted the control we thought we had over to the environment which, through selection, shapes and maintains our behavior (our "intelligence"). In the view of the phILOSophers, a scientist perceives the world around him. The action is reversed in the modern way of looking at man, which says that the environment controls man, not man the environment.

Some Common Terms Re-Defined

LIFE — What is life? Whatever it is, it could appear in *any* shape or configuration, and survive if its environment will support it. The "advanced technological civilization" the phILOSophers picture could be made up of pulsating blobs of blubber who "communicate" by belching harmful radiation. Try decoding that. Are they alive? Are we? Is there a definitive difference between organic and inorganic? Are we not committing the psychological error known as "intentionality assumption" when we attribute purpose to anything that moves?

COMMUNICATION — According to present day behavioral scientists, communication is a form of behavior. It must not be assumed that the process of coding and decoding signals from extraterrestrial civilizations is well within the range of human "intelligence". We are committing an error when we imply that universal and absolute meanings exist, even in the language and concepts of science. Anthropologists and linguists tell us that it's difficult enough, sometimes not possible, to achieve communication with our own earth languages between peoples of different cultures and value systems, let alone an alien "people" from outer space.

A series of experiments could be conducted to prove this thesis: let us see how well a group of English-speaking scientists could do in telephoning technical data to a group of Chinese-speaking scientists, without translators. We could even try the tests graphically, with a video communication system to see if we can achieve better results. We know that the results would be negative, but if we must try it to satisfy ourselves, these simple tests would not require the multi-billion dollars requested by the phILOSophers for their space message programs.

CIVILIZATION — A civilization, like a species, is selected by its adaptation to an environment. Each civilization has its own set of values and its own science. This is a kind of "cultural relativism", a point of view missed by the phILOSophers. Cultural relativism is the opposite of the missionary "chauvinism" these gentlemen are displaying when they think in terms of our own set of scientific values.

PROGRESS — The phILOSophers claim that every inhabitable planet, given enough time, will arrive at intelligence and a high technology. Here the concept of development becomes confused with progress. Development or change is not progress. The present state of our civilization is not advanced or mature or immature, and it is wrong to state otherwise.

Trap Thinking

Scientific knowledge is divided into many specialties, such as biology, physics, geology, chemistry, and so forth.

There are no hard-line boundaries between these specialties, or disciplines, as they are sometimes called; there is much overlap. For instance, deep research into chemical phenomena leads us into physics, geology pursued leads us to chemistry, and the realization that a human's limited sensory apparatus affects the results of many experiments in physics has caused physicists to become aware of biology. To better understand cultural anthropology, which is the study of the behavior of cultures, we find that we must probe into psychology, which is (supposed to be) the science of individual behavior. And psychology leads to biology, which leads us to chemistry and physics.

Are the labels of these specialties important — these specialties that we call geology, biology, physics, chemistry? We could just as well have called them tillhouse, teezee, baksheesh, and masari; chemists would still chem, biologists still bile, physicists still phyz, and geologists still geel. No matter what we called his specialty, a chemist looking at a rock might be interested in how much carbon or lead it contained. A physicist could be interested in its molecular activity, its density, or its radioactivity. A geologist would study its facets, its origin, how it was formed, and its age. A biologist could search for vestigial signs of micro-organisms. A psychologist might observe other scientists studying the rock, to determine how and why they react in reference to the rock experiments, and how their points-of-view could affect their final data. An anthropologist might study how various cultures could use the rock, such as the possible utilization of it and other rocks to construct shelters, or the possible use of it as a symbol or idol in religious ritual, or its utility as a cooking implement, or its value for the purpose of fashioning arrows and other weapons or tools.

There is a good possibility that a specialist could make wrong observations about phenomena if he is not well informed about other specialties. No matter how well he understood building trends, an architect could not tell us about the look of future cities if he knew nothing about the technology of transportation. And even if he knew where the design of buildings was heading, and all about the transportation systems of tomorrow, he would make a wrong guess if he weren't aware of the power of electronics to alter our culture's behavior, if he weren't aware of how tomorrow's inevitable full-scale three-dimensional color video-communication systems will drastically reduce our need to travel.

Let us take our myopic architect one step further. If he *were* aware of the future of electronics *and* the design of large-scale cities *and* a science of behavior to tell him about people's needs in the future, his description of the world of tomorrow would be useless if he weren't cognizant of the fact that a technocratic governance is in our future and that our money system is already on its way out, with its businessmen, lawyers, politicians, advertising agencies, economists, and accountants. Since many of the structures and artifacts in his drawings would be in error if he were not aware of this, he would have to return to the drawing board, erase the zones assigned to these obsolete functions, and start all over.

It is clear that our architect by this time would have become a careful and hesitant predictor of the future of cities — the care and caution being the product of a learning experience based on a series of errors. This explains why the more one learns from experience the more temperate or "humble" he becomes. As we accumulate knowledge our behavior substitutes awareness and a sense of perspective for dogma and foolishness. Or, to put it another way, to be a good specialist in any field we had better become good generalists and expose ourselves to the entire spectrum of scientific knowledge.

There are many examples today of experts falling into the

same error trap as our architect — a trap caused by an expertise in one narrow discipline coupled to an unawareness of the relationship of other disciplines. And there are other traps that cause errors and invalid assumptions in human affairs and science. Let us list some:

TRAP 1   Fixed and narrow views of reality based on intense specialization. Our architect's trap.

TRAP 2 Anthropomorphic and homosapiocentric projection, "God looks like a man, has feeling, is jealous, wrathful, loving, and so forth." "The earth is the center of the universe." "Social systems other than ours are immoral or wrong." "Cultures that do not have our values are strange or backward."

TRAP 3   A desire to be accepted and respected, accompanied by a fear of social sanction. Years of heavy indoctrination in a belief held by society is difficult to overturn even with clear proof of its invalidity, and could result in various forms of punishment ranging from public ridicule to harsh physical abuse. The lives of Copernicus, Galileo and Darwin furnish us with good examples of this type of social sanction. To go along with tradition rather than risk dissonance offers many material rewards, and it is the expedient course followed by many.

TRAP 4   Acculturation, the absorption of the accepted point of view of one's culture. One disadvantage of education is that it molds an individual's behavior and attitude, and stultifies his ability to see a problem from any angle other than the way of the book. The significant milestones in humanity's progress were made by people who were different, who had the advantage of less education, or who lacked the respect for textbook authority that is part of the makeup of an "educated" person. Our architect again.

TRAP 5 Language problems. Vague words such as *large*, *small*, *beautiful*, and *ugly* contribute nothing to clear communication. There are other words that are harmful blocks to a clear understanding of reality. For example, as long as we use words such as *mind, intention, purpose, drive, motivation, will,* and *creativity,* we will continue to practice psychology as witchcraft rather than as a useful science.

Trap Examples

Before Copernicus, when people believed that the earth was the center of the universe about which the sun and all the planets revolved, they were trapped in TRAP 2, with some entrapment in TRAPS 3 and 4 thrown in for good measure.

Before Darwin, when people believed that man was created as something unique and unrelated to other living organisms, they were trapped in TRAPS 2 and 5, with one foot in TRAP 3.

It is obviously foolish to rigidly assign traps, because in every given example there is overlap, and for this reason errors made by scientists are usually caused to some degree by all the traps described.

Our architect, who was trying to accurately predict the future look of cities, was trapped in TRAPS 1 and 4. A fat man who says that tightrope walking is impossible is basing his statement upon his own limited top-heavy abilities. He is hopelessly mired in TRAP 2.

Those who refuse to assign credit to any successful achievement in science by the Soviet Union or the Chinese People's Republic are viewing the world from TRAP 3. In this class of error we also find the mass of those writers, journalists, movie producers, and television celebrities who would rather "sell, not tell", by exploiting the public with popular pap designed to lull and titillate rather than inform or point to a truth.

An amusing illustration of TRAP 3 took place during the 18th century, at a meeting of the European commission to secure uniformity on weights and measures. Antoine Lavoisier, the father of the metric system, was eager to launch the method as a new standard for Europe. During the conference on metrification, in order to avoid resistance and possible rejection, he was every inch a diplomat — or, as it became, every centimeter.

A good example of TRAP 4 thinking: Remember those esteemed and highly respected men of medicine, members of the French Academy, who resisted the germ theory for years and held Louis Pasteur up to ridicule? Darwin ran into the same resistance by the distinguished scientists of his day.

Many examples of TRAP 5 errors are to be found in the field of psychology today. What should be approached as a science of human behavior with the same techniques used in physics and engineering is bogged down in an absurd archaic jargon which erroneously assigns to man a non-existent ghost or golem, who steers his physical body through life. The language that is absorbed by students of "humanistic" psychology is not representative of anything in the real world and is not verifiable. Another example of TRAP 5 is found when we utter the word *gravity* in answer to the question of what makes things fall. If the questioner accepts our answer and says, "Oh, I see," then he is a TRAP 5 citizen and easily satisfied with a sound instead of a description. Note that we really didn't tell the questioner anything — we could have answered *majnoon* and he would have been just as happy.

The words *free enterprise, money, value,* and *wealth,* are other examples of TRAP 5 pitfalls, taken from the field of economics. The word *economics* is itself an acoustic sound with no meaning in the real world. If the word *economics* was discarded for all time and the production and distribution of goods and services were controlled by systems engineers, one of the most serious problems of our time could be solved overnight, and the words *poverty deprivation*, and *scarcity* would no longer have any meaning.

The phILOSophers TRAPS

Scientists who talk about "communicating" with "intelligent civilizations" somewhere in space are speaking to us from TRAPS 1, 2, 3 and 5. TRAP 1 because they are mostly astronomers, physicists and biologists (now called exobiologists, specialists in extraterrestrial life) who are not aware of the important implications of modern behaviorism. Radical behaviorists are defining *intelligence* and *knowing* in a new difficult-to-grasp way — as behavior under the control of the environment. They clearly demonstrate that man cannot *know* the world if he is part of it. The premise of the phILOSophers is that man is standing outside the universe observing it and that others somewhere may be doing the same, and one day, if we search long enough with our giant radio telescopes, we will make contact and share all the knowledge we have gathered from our careful observations of the universe outside of our skin. And the aliens, if their technology has surpassed ours, will answer many of our questions about the riddle of the universe and tell us how to avoid inflation and optimize the profit in our profit system. That is TRAP 1 and TRAP 2 thinking. Among the trapped people in that science fiction trap are the movie makers and writers who either operate out of ignorance (pure TRAP 2), or cynically exploit the public in their efforts to maximize book sales and cinema box office receipts.

Words, words: *purpose, advanced, intelligence, man's superior brain, communications*, words without correlates in the real world. Statements such as the following, taken out of the *Stanford/NASA/AMES Research Center Report on Project CYCLOPS*, the multi-billion dollar system proposal for detecting extraterrestrial intelligent life,

should provide the reader with much fun classifying the
traps from which they arise:

1. "One of the consequences of such extensive
heavenly discourse would be the accumulation by all
participants of an enormous body of knowledge
handed down from race to race, from the beginning of
the communication phase. Included (in the Galactic
heritage) would be astronomical data dating from
several aeons ago, perhaps pictures of our own and
neighboring galaxies taken by long-dead races that
would make plain the origin and fate of the universe."
*It would be comforting to know that there are "races"
around that are able to observe and record the fate of the
universe. One wonders where they are sitting with
respect to the universe as it goes through its birth and
death cycles. Those "pictures" would be interesting to
view also.*

2. "Far more important in the long run than the
'synchronization' of the scientific development of the
cultures in contact would be: the end of the cultural
isolation of the human race, its entry as a participant
in the community of intelligent species everywhere,
and the development of a spirit of adult pride in man,
rather than childish rivalry among men." *We are at a
loss to understand how eliminating childish rivalry can
result in a spirit of adult pride, all because of participation in a community of intelligent species.*

That last quotation reveals an unawareness of the fact
that what we know as a human is an organism whose
repertoire of behavior is a dependent variable continually
controlled by, and changing with, the independent variable
that is the environment. And the quotation is also a classic
example of TRAP 2 anthropomorphic projection.

3. "A more subtle and plausible risk is that an alien culture, under the guise of teaching or helping us, might cause us to build devices that would enable the alien culture to gain control over us. A computer-controlled experiment in biochemistry, for example, might be used to create their life form here. There is no limit to the kind of threats one can imagine, given treachery on their part and vulnerability on ours. Appropriate security measures and a healthy degree of suspicion are the only weapons." *Anthropomorphic projection is one thing, but to project our hostility into an "alien race" could easily turn us into a red-necked Earth teeming with air raid wardens. On the other hand, if we can convince the government that such a risk does exist, imagine what that could do for our economy — more defense contracts that would put everybody happily to work and eliminate forever the danger of a peace. Sometimes this kind of a quotation from an engineering and science source is a self-justification for spending (other people's) money to allow these technical types to carry on with their "research".*

4. "Regardless of the morphology of other intelligent beings, their microscopes, telescopes, communication systems and power plants must have been at some time in their history almost indistinguishable in working principles from ours." *Now our aliens have a sense of vision and peep through microscopes and telescopes and communicate with one another just as we do.*

The following is from an editorial by Norman Cousins on the subject of Project Cyclops, taken from the *Saturday Review* of November 30, 1974: "If the (Cyclops) project does not bear fruit . . . . . we should make a continuing

committment beyond that time as long as may be necessary
. . . . ." Here is a case of not learning from your errors. Even if
it doesn't work, we should carry on forever.

The following two citations are an example of direct
contradiction in the point of view of a popular scientist:

  1. "The biology on other planets is, of course,
expected to be different from our own." Carl Sagan,
Scientific American, May 1975.

  2. "The plaque on Pioneer 10 is (the sort) of picture
which transmitted as an object on a spacecraft or as a
picture by radio transmission, would be reliably
understood by an advanced extraterrestrial
civilization." Carl Sagan, *The Cosmic Connection.*

Gerard K. O'Neill, an expert in the field of high-energy
particle physics, is also recognized as the world's leading
authority on space colonization. He is trapped in all the
TRAPS in *The High Frontier:*

"We are in the midst of a knowledge explosion, and if our
rate of acquisition of new scientific knowledge continues to
accelerate, as it is now doing, it seems to me quite likely that
within much less than a thousand years we will know, if not
everything about the natural world, at least so much that
science will no longer be of great interest and challenge. In
that case I would expect that our most talented individuals,
a few of whom now study the natural and biological
sciences, would turn their attention to the arts, or to the
greatest intellectual problem that is now imaginable to
me: the *riddle of consciousness.* My picture of an advanced
civilization is one in which science, aided by computers
with an intelligence level far higher than that of any living
being, will already have answered all the *merely physical*
questions. Some individuals may take part in direct
exploration and exploitation of new star systems, slowly
spreading the culture of their species in an expanding
sphere from their parent star. I consider it probable,
though, that in the advanced stages of a long-lived

civilization the *physical world will be taken for granted, as something long since understood and thoroughly tamed. Most of the interest and activity, I would guess, will be intellectual, artistic, and social.*"

The above citation is italicized in three places, in order to identify the trouble spots in the thinking of this scientist. The *riddle of consciousness* he refers to is apparently something non-physical, a spiritual remainder left over after we arrive at the point of "knowing everything" and "science will no longer be of great interest and challenge."

The term *merely physical* could only mean that he believes there is also a non-physical world — a spiritual immanence beyond the reach of science. It is difficult to believe that these are the words of a physicist. This same thought is repeated in the third statement: *"the physical world will be taken for granted, as something long since understood and thoroughly tamed. Most of the interest and activity I would guess, will be intellectual, artistic, and social."* When we know everything, we can then sit around and philosophize, paint, play musical instruments, write poetry, and socialize.

Here are two scientists addressing us (unbelievably) from TRAP 2:

> **Scientist 1:** "Knowledge of our language will enable the (alien) probe to tell us many fascinating things: the physics and chemistry of the next hundred years, wonders of astrophysics yet unknown to man, beautiful mathematics. After a while it may supply us with outstanding breakthroughs in biology and medicine. But first we will have to tell it a lot about our biological makeup. Perhaps it will write poetry or discuss philosophy. *Perhaps the messenger knows how the universe started, whether it will end, and what will happen then.* Maybe the probe knows what it all means, but I wonder ..... I think that is why Superon

wants to consult us." (Emphasis added.) *The Galactic Club*, by Ronald N. Bracewell, Stanford University.

Scientist 2: "I can imagine, in such a galaxy, great civilizations growing up near the black holes, with the planets from black holes designated as farm worlds, ecological preserves, vacations and resorts, specialty manufacturers, outposts for poets and musicians, and retreats for those who do not cherish big-city life. The discovery of such a galactic culture might happen at any moment — for example, by radio signals sent to the Earth from civilizations on planets of other stars. Such a discovery might not occur for many centuries, until a lone small vehicle from Earth approaches a nearby black hole and there discovers the usual array of buoys to warn off improperly outfitted spacecraft, and encounters the local immigration officers, among whose duties it is to explain the transportation conventions to newly arrived yokels from emerging civilizations." *The Cosmic Connection*, Carl Sagan.

Sagan has another word for what we call TRAP 2. He calls it *chauvinism*. His term is as useful as ours because it means the same thing. But in spite of his awareness of the trap of chauvinism he couldn't help but fall into it, as demonstrated by the preceding quote, and by the drawings of Earthman and Earthwoman on the plaque now riding on Pioneer 10. He speaks of oxygen chauvinism, the erroneous belief that extraterrestrial organisms must have oxygen to survive. We agree with him, just as we do when he speaks of temperature chauvinism, carbon chauvinism, and even planetary chauvinism, but he hasn't taken it far enough. He forgot about life chauvinism — that idea that life elsewhere must satisfy our own earth-bound "intelligence" requirements. The idea that intelligent life, *by earth definitions*, must exist somewhere else in the universe is the ultimate expression of chauvinism.

Wire-Clinging Behavior

The following is an exercise to help us lose our anthro-pocentricity: Little is known about earth-bound life. About three hundred thousand types of plants and over a million different species of animals have been classified so far; there are about a million more life forms on earth still to be discovered. It is estimated that almost a billion different types of organisms have lived on earth, and only about one percent of now-living organisms have been chemically analyzed.

Considering all of that, man as we know him reduces to an insignificant part of the matter-in-motion that we call *life*. The term *matter-in-motion* is also a case of anthropomorphic projection, for there are "live" forms that are virtually immobile: the African lung fish, a nearly closed system, can survive for a period of four years out of water in a state of ambiosis. It just stops ticking.

How about energy eaters like plants who feed partially on sunlight, and plants that digest insects, like the Venus flytrap? And sexless organisms like the banded flamefish that possess both male and female organs? They can produce eggs and the sperm to fertilize them, and can propagate with a mate. And the "intelligence" of the protozoa *paramecium aurelia*, which has been "taught", or conditioned, in a classic experiment, to cling to a platinum wire when deprived of food, because previously they had learned to cling to the wire when it was coated with food? Purely a mechanical phenomenon, but difficult to see as other than intelligence.

Our intelligence, awareness, and observation of the universe is, in reality, a process similar to the wire-clinging behavior of the paramecia. Perhaps it is more complex, but it is conceptually the same thing — what we call intelligence is behavior controlled and shaped by the environment. Everything in nature depends on, is moved by, and owes its existence to, the world around it. Man is no exception. A person engaged in what appears to be a very advanced and complex endeavor, scientific research, is performing another form of wire clinging.

The urge to project *will* and *motivation* into the clinging behavior of the paramecium is what gets us into trouble. Just as we know that an apple doesn't fall from a tree because it *desires* to get to the ground, the paramecium does not *desire* to cling to the wire, and any other organism does not *desire* to perform any act.

One who views another human and sees a human instead of a complex machine, is seeing in the same way a poet sees when he looks at a jet aircraft. Only an aircraft engineer and aerodynamicist can "see" a modern airplane. We must "know" to see.

Acoustic Behavior

Verbal communication between humans (which should be termed "verbal behavior") appears to be fraught with "knowledge" and "awareness", but is in reality wire-clinging behavior. A human soon learns that uttering the sounds "please get me an apple" is easier than crossing the room and going through all the operations necessary to get an apple. But the phenomenon is culture- and space-locked. It would not work to say "get me an apple" to a Russian who did not understand English. Imagine again the Chinese scientist who couldn't speak English trying to converse with an American scientist who did not understand Chinese. How much "communication" would take place? Zero. Now imagine scientists trying to communicate ideas with other species of animals and plants. The problem magnifies, to say the least.

Next, let us imagine Earth scientists using pictures to "communicate" with "scientists" on another planet who are biologically different; no eyes, ears, hands, or mouths. Impossible, even if we accept their limited definition of "communication". You say nothing is impossible? Well, it is impossible, without modification, to make an automobile fly. Only if we decided not to call it an automobile or an airplane is it possible to make an automobile fly. It is our language that fogs the issue. For the same reason, it is impossible for man to see a germ without a sensory aid such as a microscope. It is impossible to "communicate" with a pulsating blob of blubber belching harmful radiation, which may be the form of life on another planet. It is also impossible for that blubber to "communicate" with us. It can certainly affect us, as we could probably affect it. If you want to call that "communication", then we must redefine the term.

Men *affect* each other's behavior with acoustics and graphic techniques. There is no *delivery of information*. Speech is an acoustic phenomenon, not a data communication system. The computer analogy applied to man gets us into trouble. There is no evidence of memory storage in man as in a computer; what appears to be memory is changed behavior. When we say a person "searches" his memory for a forgotten name, we are saying that there is an internal eye rummaging through a file system. That is not true. When we say we "picture" something in our heads, we are mistakenly implying there is a picture we are looking at with an internal eye. All the head and brain surgery in the world would not reveal evidence of a picture, a movie screen, or a memory file. When we say we are thinking, our vocal apparatus is usually operating in a non-obvious, covert manner — below the whisper level. In reality, most thinking involves talking to ourselves. Other kinds of "thinking" involve muscular activity, or unseen behavior.

Behavior And Evolution

If the paramecia didn't learn to go after food, they would not exist, and there would be nothing to talk about as far as those paramecia were concerned. If the earth were a little colder we would not exist. So let us add to the many billions of life forms that have existed the many trillions (at least) that *could have* existed if conditions were otherwise, then we have a picture of the random, mindless universe. (The word *random* is not correct. In the cosmos, *random equals design.)*

We do not have two arms with which to do things; we do things *because* we have two arms. It appears that the giraffe was *designed* with a long neck because his food grew high. But no. He was a mutant who happened to fit the high-growing food situation. If he didn't, he wouldn't be around for us to talk about.

Many mutants never made it. Many existing life forms barely make it. That is what Darwin gave us — freak births or mutations take place continually. If the environment can support them, they survive. If not, they are not here for us to observe. Consequently, it all looks so perfect because all we can observe are those who made it. The universe appears to run with clock-like precision. No matter how the universe ran, it would always appear perfect. If all the planets were cube-shaped and moved in square erratic orbits, we would still say "how perfect, how planned, how precision". In any form it would work "perfectly".

The acquiring of behavior works *similar to Darwin's natural selection, but on a smaller scale.* It is just as "random" as the development of the species: some of it is supported by its environment (reinforced), some of it is snuffed out (extinguished). As he grows, a human's behavior is shaped and strengthened by his exposure to his culture and other factors in his environment, similar to natural selection, but on a smaller time scale. Of course he begins life with a genetic endowment that is the product of aeons of shaping, through the process of selection, by the environment.

Since it is not possible to objectively observe a phenomenon (that is, from *no* point of view) we find ourselves always in a trap of one kind or another. Scientific progress in one sense is a progression of climbing out of traps to higher ground, to less limiting traps. Or to put it another way, science progresses by moving toward a more generalized perspective, seeing relationships, and avoiding dogma and false language.

The boyish enthusiasm, full of awe and science fiction wonder, with which the cereal box scientists write and lecture betrays an ignorance of the complexity of the communication process. To whom are they talking? Earthbound schizophrenics live in another kind of reality and are incommunicado to the sort of "thinking" that is going on around them. When these scientists write, they are committing anthropomorphic errors, talking to themselves, assuming that somebody out there is sharing their awareness. Just as the attitude of a well trained and skillful psychiatrist or therapist should be objective, clinical, removed from the patient, and in a sense manipulative, so should a scientist with a world view be unabsorbed in the "excitement of his discoveries".

The height of crass commercialism, and a revelation of the depths to which some scientists are involved in the money system, is revealed by the following quotation from *The Cosmic Connection* by Sagan: "Another viewpoint worth considering is space exploration as entertainment. A Viking-Mars lander could be completely funded through the sale, to every American, of a single issue of a magazine containing pictures taken on the surface of Mars by Viking. Photographs of the earth, the moon, the planets, and spiral and irregular galaxies are an appropriate and even characteristic art form of our age. Such novel and oddly moving photographs as the Lunar Orbiter image of the interior of the crater Copernicus and the *Mariner IX* photography of the Martian volcanos, wind streaks, moons, and polar ice caps speak both to a sense of wonder and to a sense of art. An unmanned roving vehicle on Mars could probably be supported by subscription television. A phonograph record of the output of a microphone on Mars, where there seems to be a great deal of acoustic energy, might have wide sales."

In order to understand a mountain, its formation, and its configuration, one has to look at it analytically as a geologist does. There is no harm in looking at a mountain as a poet does, but his view of a mountain will never be useful to mankind, because he will never understand it to the point of being able to control and utilize it to prolong and better human life. There is more humanism in prolonging human life than in a poem. The same error is caused by talk about communication. To look for communication, to see communication everywhere between men, and between mankind and visitors from out there, is to miss the point. If we looked at communications as a geologist looks at a mountain, the fallacy would disappear.

The Language of Science

It is becoming increasingly obvious that we have come to a crossroads. Confusion in science and world unrest are examples of this crossroads. Archaic language has shaped our point-of-view; and is an important influence in our cultures, customs, mores, institutions, science, artifacts, and points-of-view about science. We must understand the power of the environment to shape us, especially our language environment. Most of the problems of the phILOSophers are verbal; their language reflects the structure of our past history. It is a vicious circle — archaic viewpoints shape the structure of our language and vice versa. This is why the language of science is mathematics, our most efficient technique for representing universal processes.

We must look at the world as a process made up of transformals and invariants. *Transformals* means change, *invariants* means permanence, or lack of change. Just as the world is made up of matter and non-matter, depending on how we look at it, the universe is infinitely dense and at the same time reveals itself as infinitely empty as we tear away material to look for the basic stuff from which it is made. Someone once suggested that no behavioral scientist could actually perform his task well unless he was a skilled student of mathematics. While that may not be completely true, if that point-of-view were broadened to include all science, we could understand how language other than mathematics can lead us into trouble. The lack of linguistic rigor is one of the problems in the communication of popular science today. Mathematics teaches us to use structural premises, called postulates, but we are also taught to never consider them "true".

Mathematics also teaches us to make no claims. The behavior of all organisms and the processes of all the universe are similar in structure, and based on mathematical theories of statistics and probability. Boole, in his *Laws of Thought*, broadened mathematics to include what he called "logic", in connection with probability theory, and the Uncertainty Principle of Heisenberg was, and still is, a revolutionary general principle. Heisenberg's point, simplified, is that we can never observe phenomena in nature objectively because our method of observation always affects what we observe. For instance, lighting an experiment to observe the behavior of certain viruses affects their behavior, yet we cannot observe them without illumination. But then how are things supposed to behave "objectively"?

Mathematics, the language of science, is beautiful in its honesty and uncomplexity. The languages of our planet, so complex and vague that they will always evade analysis, remain fundamentally at the root of most of the problems of the phILOSophers and in the relationships of humans to each other.

With Almost
2   Absolute Certainty

"At this very minute, with almost absolute certainty, radio waves sent forth by other intelligent civilizations are falling on earth."*

> Frank D. Drake, Professor of
> Astronomy, Cornell Univ.
> *Intelligent Life in Space*

Contemporary scientific interest in interstellar communication began with a giant exercise in anthropocentrism in a 1959 paper published in *Nature*, authored by Cocconi and Morrison. Other scientists soon fell into the same trap, and papers began to appear by Dyson, Drake, Bracewell, Oliver, Huang, Handelsman, Shklovskii, Sagan, and others. S.H. Dole's major work on habitable planets appeared soon after, and was followed by the popular books of Drake and Sullivan. An extensive bibliography was also published by Hughes Research Labs. Their premises for the plausibility of technologically advanced life are taken from the Project Cyclops report released by NASA (comments in parenthesis added).

---

*"With almost absolute certainty" should take its place in the lexicon of ambiguous phrases along with "benign neglect" and "unqualified maybe". "With almost absolute certainty" makes anything almost certainly right.

Their premises follow:

1. Planetary systems are the rule rather than the exception. (For the purpose of argument we agree that this may be a fact.)

2. The origin and early evolution of life on earth is explicable in terms of the basic laws of physics and chemistry. (We agree.)

3. The laws of physics and chemistry apply throughout the universe. (The laws of physics and chemistry are not immutable. It is true that all phenomena in the universe are lawful, but we might be startled by the laws we will encounter as we delve deeper into the realm of physical science. Today's laws are to be broken tomorrow.)

4. On Earth, intelligence leads to attempts to modify and utilize the environment, which is the beginning of technology. This kind of intelligence seems a highly probable one on any earth-like planet. (They have it backwards: the environment modifies and controls the organism. The kind of control that the organism has over the environment is environmentally controlled.)

They next state that technological systems are shaped more by the physical laws of optics, thermodynamics, electromagnetics, or other reactions on which they are based than by the nature of the beings that design them. (This is fallacious. Technological systems reflect the behavior of organisms in response to their environment. They are shaped by organisms who are in turn shaped by the environment.)

They go on to say that we need not worry much over the problem of exchanging information between them and us. (Let's try it first between us and the dolphins, or between two human beings, one Chinese and one English.)

Their terminology, the terms they use, like *race, alien civilizations, interstellar communication, transmitting their history and knowledge, their advanced cultures*, are examples of woolly-headed thinking, using distortive non-scientific language which has no meaning in the real world. They "postulate" that interstellar communications, having spread rapidly throughout the Galaxy once it began, is now a reality for countless races, and participation in this linked community of intelligent beings confers advantages that greatly outweigh the obligations. (That statement is full of childish non-science too elementary to be taken seriously.)

PhILOSophy is anthropomorphism and anthropocentrism at its most heightened example. The phILOSophers are looking for other astronomers and scientists out there who would be willing to share the secrets of the universe. They never consider the possibility of contacting others who may be parallel to us in their development; never do they discuss the possibility of civilizations who might be behind us; never do they describe a landscape like ours, with crime, violence, and corruption. That would be laughable. But science fiction minds are well-satisfied with a picture of a futuristic society.

Most of the Cyclops report is technical, describing electromagnetic communication techniques, acquisition and search problems, antenna elements, the receiver system, signal processing, and the like. It goes on to describe the search strategy and the possibility of using Cyclops as a research tool. This is all very well and good, and to be respected, as it is the reporting of some very knowledgeable scientists in the field, but it is a perfect example of doing a faulty thing well, because the entire concept is fallacious.

The phILOSophers are indulging in a classic example of anthropomorphic projection, the same kind of reasoning that makes God into man's image. When they speak of "intelligent beings" out there, they are implying that these "people", no matter how biologically different they tell us they may be, are warm, chatty, pipe-smoking intellectual-scientists who may be ready to "communicate" with us about our mutual problems — thus creating beings on other planets made into our own image.

Man's biology is the result of more than a billion years of mutation and selection. The process is one of editorship rather than authorship — the selection or rejection by the environment of a virtually infinite variety of behaviors, shapes, and sizes submitted for consideration. Should all life disappear from the earth and begin again from so-called "inorganic" material, there is virtually no chance at all that a species similar to man would occur again. Should only man disappear, the chance of another human evolving from the remaining life forms is zero. There is no good reason to suppose that it could happen again, here or anywhere else.

Lost in the Land of Oz

Astronomer Frank Drake launched a sensational attempt in April, 1959, to contact extraterrestrial intelligence. He arrived at the National Radio Astronomy Observatory at Greenbank, West Virginia, in April, 1958, as a staff member of the new National Observatory and soon after convinced the observatory administration to let him use the big 85-inch radio telescope to scan the Cosmos for messages from a highly advanced society. One of the most respected astronomers of our time, Otto Struve, then director of the observatory at Greenbank, wrote of Frank Drake's project: "I believe that science has reached the point where it is necessary to take into account the action of intelligent beings in addition to the classical laws of physics."

Drake called his search *Project Ozma*, named after the Land of Oz, a difficult-to-reach place, peopled with strange beings.

At a symposium on astronomy at Colgate University, Drake said: "In view of the continuous formation of stars, there should be a continued emergence of technically proficient civilizations."

The project began at 4 a.m. on April 8th, 1960, aiming at Tau Ceti, the first recorded event of man listening for signals from extraterrestrial civilizations. No emissions were received, so that afternoon they decided to aim at another star, Epsilon Eridani. The loudspeaker and the needle on the recorder went wild with high-speed pulses whose frequency was so stable that it could only be coming from an intelligent civilization. For the next five minutes Drake and his associates were charged with excitement. Then the signal stopped. Two weeks later it was confirmed that the source of the transmissions was an earth-bound United States military experiment in radar countermeasures using airborne transmitters. The project was halted after a few more months because of the need for the telescope in other projects.

From Humility to Dogma

While this was going on, Ronald N. Bracewell stated in an article in *Nature* that other civilizations would probably not use radio signals to contact other planets but, instead, would use automated messengers to orbit a star while waiting for its planetary civilizations to become technically advanced enough to understand its communication.

Bracewell said, "It is conceivable that some remote community could breed a sub-race of space messengers, brains without bodies or limbs, storing the traditions of their society, mostly to be expended fruitlessly, but some destined to be the instruments of the spread of intra-galactic culture." Also, "Should we be surprised if the beginning of its message were a television image of a constellation?" (TRAP 2.)

Carl Sagan, in a paper presented to the American Rocket Society in November, 1962, said that: "Other civilizations, aeons more advanced than ours, must today be plying the spaces between the stars." He argued that radio telescopy was an inferior way of making contact because it does not allow us to exchange artifacts. "Interstellar space flight sweeps away these difficulties." (TRAP 2.)

Edward Purcell, the Nobel prize winner who discovered the 21-centimeter line in the radio spectrum, stated in a lecture at Brookhaven National Laboratory on Long Island: "We haven't grown up to it. It is a project which has to be funded by the *century*, not by the fiscal year. Furthermore, it is a project which is very likely to fail *completely* if you spend a lot of money and go around every ten years and say 'We haven't heard anything yet'. You can imagine how you'd make out before a Congressional committee, but I think it is not too soon to have the fun of thinking about it. And I think it is a much less childish subject to think about than astronautical space travel. In my view, most of the projects of the Space Cadets are not really imaginative . . . . . All this stuff about travelling around the universe in space suits — except for *local* exploration (within the solar system) which I have not discussed — belongs back where it came from — on the cereal box."

Here is Ronald Bracewell again, in a lecture at the University of Sydney, where he wondered whether space beings would want our gold or would they want us as slaves? But then he answered that if they were smart enough to get here they probably didn't need our gold! (Exclamation added.)

Freeman Dyson, of the Institute of Advanced Study, at Princeton, in a letter to *Scientific American* in 1964, stated: "Intelligence may indeed be a benign influence creating isolated groups of philosopher-kings far apart in the heavens and enabling them to share at leisure their accumulated wisdom." (Deeply trapped in TRAP 2.)

Here is a quotation from Father Angelo Secchi, the highly regarded Jesuit astronomer, taken from *We Are Not Alone* by Walter Sullivan, an excellent chronicle of the search for intelligent life in space: "It would seem absurd to find uninhabited deserts in these limitless regions. No! These worlds are bound to be populated by creatures capable of recognizing, honoring, and loving their creator." (Another trapped in TRAP 2.)

Harlow Shapley, the famous astronomer, from the same book, is inspired to say: "To be a participant is in itself a glory. With our confreres on distant planets; with our fellow animals and plants of land, air, and sea; with the rocks and waters of all planetary crusts, and the photons and atoms that make up the stars — with all these we are associated in an existence and an evolution that inspires respect and deep reverence. We cannot escape humility. And as groping philosophers and scientists we are thankful for the mysteries that still lie beyond our grasp." (Let the reader classify this one.)

And George Wald, professor of biochemistry at Harvard says, from the same book: "Life has a status in the physical universe. It is part of the order of nature. It has a high place in that order since it probably represents the most complex state of organization that matter has achieved in our universe. We on this planet have an especially proud place as men; *for in us as men matter has begun to contemplate itself.*" (Emphasis added. See pages 86 and 156 to identify the core of this absurdity.)

Carl Sagan, from *The Cosmic Connection:* "Organic compounds have been found in meteorites and in interstellar space. Small quantities have been found even in such an inhospitable environment as the Moon. They are suspected to exist in Jupiter, in the outer planets of the Solar System, as well as on Titan, the largest moon of Saturn." In the same vein: "The hypothesis that advanced technical civilizations exist on planets of other stars is amenable to experimental testing. It has been removed from the arena of pure speculation. It is now in the arena of experiment." (A classic case of hope-masquerading-as-fact.)

Sagan again, from the same book: "The idea of extraterrestrial life is an idea whose time has come." (He says *yes*.)

Sagan, from *Other Worlds:* "I cannot say I believe that there is life out there." (He says *no*.)

Professor George Wald is quoted in *The Galactic Club*, by Bracewell: "I think there is no question that we live in an inhabited universe that has life all over it." (The reader should note that we have progressed from humble speculation to positive dogma.)

The views of I. Shklovskii, an internationally respected Soviet astronomer, are discussed by Carl Sagan in *The Cosmic Connection:* "Since there were no signs of such an advanced civilization on Mars today, Shklovskii concluded that Phobos and possibly Deimos had been launched in the distant past by a now extinct Martian civilization." (Phobos and Deimos are the moons of Mars.)

A news release by the *Soviet News Service ZNS* in January, 1978, reported: "Dr. I. Shklovskii has told a man-in-space conference in the USSR that he now believes humans are utterly alone in the galaxy. Shklovskii claims that the evolution of intelligent life on the earth was caused by a coincidence of highly improbable circumstances. He went so far as to describe our presence as a 'miracle'. The realization that we are alone, Shklovskii says, actually places an even greater responsibility on the human race. He argues that it is up to Earthlings to spread the 'miracle' throughout the universe."

The reader should be reminded that Shklovskii is still caught in a trap with the other phILOSophers. The argument should not be whether life does or doesn't exist on other planets. The more serious error is the fundamental fallacy in the concept of intelligent life.

Ronald Bracewell, from *The Galactic Club:* "What we do not know for sure, since it has never been demonstrated, is whether an artificial machine can *think*, and until this has actually been done, many will harbor a lingering doubt." (TRAPS 1, 2, and 5.) We wonder what Dr. Bracewell thinks thinking could be. Obviously he does not realize that anything man can do can be done by a machine, *only better;* because man *is* a machine. Or, as Shklovskii puts it in his *Intelligent Life In The Universe*, written with Carl Sagan: "Cybernetics, molecular biology, and neurophysiology together will some day very likely be able to create artificial intelligent beings which hardly differ from men, except for being significantly more advanced. Such beings would be capable of self improvement and probably would be much longer-lived than conventional human beings."

Bracewell again, from *The Galactic Club:* "Perhaps there could be intelligent scum. After all, the size of the human individual has practically nothing to do with the size of his pyramids, cathedrals, oil tankers, rockets, and other products of technology. Had we been twelve-foot giants or three-foot dwarfs, would it have had any influence on the scale of such undertakings? I do not see why scum composed of single-cell plants living on a water-air interface, possessing no resistance to wind or weather, could not obtain technological control of the environment."

It takes a lot of creative imagination, even for the most open-minded scientist, to picture scum erecting a skyscraper or building a rocket. But that is not the important point. If the scum is living on a water-air interface, then the environment is in control of *it*. The behavior of all organisms is under the control of the environment at all times, unless one believes in the spontaneous generation of behavior, or some other form of magic.

Of Dolphins and Space Aliens

In 1961, the Space Science Board of the National Academy of Sciences held a conference at the National Radio Astronomy Observatory to discuss the possibility of communication with extraterrestrial intelligence. The conference was attended by:

Dana Atchley, Jr., President of Microwave Associates, a specialist in microwave communications.

Giuseppe Cocconi, the gentleman who was responsible for the beginning of all the interest in extraterrestrial communications and who had originally proposed a search for signals on the 21-centimeter wave length.

Su-Shu Huang, who was responsible for calculating what type of stars would be habitable for living organisms.

Philip Morrison, co-author with Cocconi of the article in Nature Magazine which generated the initial interest in a search through the universe for other forms of life.

Carl Sagan, probably the most popular of the phILOSophers.

Otto Struve, the director of the National Radio Astronomy Observatory.

Melvin Calvin, Nobel Prize winner in chemistry, who had worked out the chemical processes by which life might evolve from so-called inanimate matter.

Frank Drake, the initiator of the first search through the universe with microwave receivers on the 21-centimeter band using the 85-foot antenna at the National Radio Astronomy Observatory.

John Lilly, the world's foremost authority on the dolphin, specializing in the techniques of communication between man and the dolphin.

Bernard Oliver, then Vice President for research and development at the Hewlett/Packard Company.

At the meeting, Lilly discussed the "intelligence" of dolphins. "It is probable that their intelligence is comparable to ours, though in a very strange fashion." He then talked about the possibility of exploiting the intelligence of dolphins. For instance, dolphins could be used by a country to seek out the submarines of another country or they could help rescue the pilots of downed military planes. Or dolphins could serve on a demolition team, of course hoping they would be loyal to our side. (Notice the stress on the military uses of dolphin technology.) Lilly went on to say that they could also be used to sneak bombs into the harbors of the enemy. Then Lilly mentioned that they could possibly turn out to be pacifists and not be trainable from that point of view. (Hell no — we won't go.) Maybe they could also be used in psychological warfare, Lilly went on, and could be persuaded to "shout something into the listening ear" of hostile submarines. (Lilly's work has been questioned by other dolphin experts, their research indicating that there may be little, if any, basis for his theory that dolphins have a language of their own. There is not enough data on the sounds that dolphins make to support Lilly's language theory, and there is doubt among some experts about Lilly's contention that he had taught dolphins to mimic words.)

Then Lilly said something that terminated his speech with a thought that almost seemed to agree with the point of this book, at least in minor detail. He said that to communicate with other species on earth was similar to the problem of communicating with other species on another planet, but it would take "a very long time (and) a lot of research" to prove that this is not possible. So he ended his talk with the point that communication with intelligent life elsewhere was to be a difficult matter. After Lilly's talk, Frank Drake presented the meeting with an equation which was written on the blackboard:

$$N = R^* \, f_p \, n_e \, f_l \, f_i \, f_c \, {}^*L$$

That equation was supposed to mean the following: The letter N represents the number of civilizations out there that are capable of communicating with other solar systems at the present time. All of the symbols on the right side of the equation are the factors that affect this number. When multiplied together they would give us the number of alien societies with which we can possibly communicate.

Let us examine the factors that appear on the right side of the equation, as Frank Drake defined them:

R^* The rate that stars were being formed in the galaxy during the period the solar system was born. This would tell us the number of stars in the galaxy near which intelligent life may have reached advanced technological development in the past few hundred millions of years. The attendees at the meeting agreed that a conservative estimate would be about one new star per year.

f_p The fraction of stars with planets. The assumption here is that when a star is formed the material that is left over either becomes a twin star or a system of rotating planets about the star and since half the stars that we see are two-star systems, we can assume that the other half have planets. The leftover material may not become planets however, but may be disposed of by being blown off into space. If that possibility is correct, then the fraction of stars with planets could be a minimum of one fifth.

n_e The number of planets, or solar systems, with an environment suitable for life. The estimate here is that for this galaxy the number lies between one and five.

f_l The fraction of suitable planets on which life actually appears. The group agreed that this number would amount to one.

f_l The fraction of life-bearing planets on which intelligence emerges. The conference attendees decided that the number one should be assigned to this because they felt that intelligence would eventually evolve on any planet which bears life.

f_c The fraction of intelligent societies that develop the ability and desire to communicate with other worlds. Morrison, lecturing to the Philosophical Society of Washington, suggested that technologically advanced societies in space are already contacting each other. He said that they have already solved the life histories of the stars and many of the universe's secrets, and since they knew so much, the only thing left to explore would be the experience of others. "What are their novels?" he asked, "What are their art histories? What are the anthropological problems of those distant stars? That is the kind of material that these remote philosophers have been stewing over for a long time." Morrison went on to say what if "they turn into some other animal and are not interested anymore?" (It is hard to believe that those statements could be uttered by a scientist.) At any rate, the attendees agreed that from one tenth to one fifth of intelligent species would attempt to signal other planets.

L   The longevity of each technology in the communicative state. Sagan estimated that one in 100,000 stars have planets with advanced technological societies in orbit around them. The attendees decided that the figure is either less than 1000 years or more than 100 million years.

A year later, in 1962, Sagan, in a lecture to the American Rocket Society, stated that space travel was superior to communication with radio waves. He said that "other civilizations, aeons more advanced than ours, must today be plying the spaces between the stars." His point was that radio does not permit contact between technologically advanced civilizations and one that is not quite that advanced, that does not possess radio technology. And one of the limitations of radio communications is that it doesn't allow us to exchange products and artifacts. "Interstellar space flight sweeps away these difficulties. It reopens the arena of action for civilizations where local exploration has been completed; it provides access beyond the planetary frontiers, where the opportunities are limitless." And then he went on to point out that the fuel problem could be solved by an "interstellar ram jet", one that would scoop up hydrogen enroute.

Then he said that "a central galactic information repository" may exist where all the knowledge of these advanced civilizations is collected, providing information access for others (something like the main reading room of the N.Y. Public Library). He suggested that such advanced societies are probably sending out expeditions and returning, some with negative reports on the other solar systems visited and some with positive reports of civilizations. "The wealth, diversity, and brilliance of this commerce," he said, "the exchange of goods and information, of arguments and artifacts, of concepts and conflicts, must continuously sharpen the curiosity and enhance the vitality of the participating societies."

Sagan proposed that scouts from these advanced civilizations may have visited the earth in the past — perhaps 10,000 times in our past history. He suggested that our myths and legends should be re-analyzed for evidence of visits from other planets, recommending that the *Book of the Secrets of Enoch* which is also known as the *Slavonic Enoch*, and reportedly written by biblical figures, should be investigated. In the book, Enoch visited seven heavens and observed many wonders, among which were flying creatures with characteristics of lions and the heads of crocodiles. In the seventh heaven he met God, who let him in on all the secrets of the universe. Enoch was told how the earth and all the planets were created, and recorded all of this in 366 books; and when he returned to earth, sought to deliver his wisdom to mankind.

Frank Drake stated that there is a similar tale in the first three chapters of Ezekiel, in the Bible, where the prophet is visited by four winged creatures and miraculously conveyed to the captive Israelites.

Sagan suggested that another ancient legend should be analyzed critically and that is the report by Berosus, which describes how civilization came to Sumeria. Berosus, who was a Babylonian priest and lived about 280 B.C., recorded the story of the flood and creation. Sagan expressed doubt that these legends had anything to do with visits by alien creatures but he insisted that we should continue to analyze the records because one day we might find evidence of a more exotic visit. He also said "it was not out of the question" that relics of alien visits may still be found, and that one day, perhaps, we may discover a hidden base on the far side of the moon.

Frank Drake is another phILOSopher who insists that such early visitors could possibly have left their artifacts right here on our planet. Drake said that to preserve these artifacts they might have been cached in limestone caves, but he appeared to disagree with the feasibility of the space travel idea because he calculated that to transmit one pulse, one bit of information, 1000 light years by radio would cost only 5¢. Travel through space would be highly uneconomical.

Poor Ideas Carried Out Well

Years ago in the early experimental days of aviation, daring inventors devised many novel approaches to the problems of flight. One of these was a machine, cleverly conceived, and literally designed to lift itself by its bootstraps.

Mounted about 10 feet above a conventional fuselage was a large hollow dome, supported by struts. The airplane had no wings, it was simply a fuselage with the umbrella-like sheet metal dome mounted above. Housed in the interior of the aircraft was a high-pressure air supply whose exit nozzle was aimed at the underside of the dome. The idea was that a high-speed concentrated blast of air, expelled from the aircraft and delivered to the dome, would lift the plane into the air, and by controlling the blast pressure and direction, the airplane could be made to rise, lower, and tilt in any direction.

There was a lot of excitement on the day of the test flight, with newsreel cameramen and the press ready to record a historic event. The inventor stood proudly to one side as the test pilot took his place in the cockpit and the cameras ground busily away. Of course we know the result — it was like trying to raise yourself into the air while sitting in a chair, by grabbing the bottom of the chair and lifting. Or like pushing against the front of a rowboat while seated in it, to make it go forward.

Where there is action there is reaction. At the first blast of air, which was set for maximum thrust at lift-off, the umbrella-like dome separated from the fuselage and fell to the ground. The inventor shook his head sadly and walked off, probably headed back to the drawing board.

What can we learn from this event? The craft was well designed, properly stress-analyzed, and its structure and dynamics were an example of sound aircraft engineering. But the fundamental physics of the idea was fallacious. Which means that a fundamentally fallacious idea can be carried out well. Our inventor was clever, but what he was doing was not. *There have been many well-thought-out concepts in science, presented in impressive jargon, that have been ultimately discarded because of their fallacious basis.*

Such a concept is the "science" that has been created by the phILOSophers. The literature is impressive. Their books are voluminous and properly fattened by long chapters reviewing what is already known about the solar system and living organisms. Some of the volumes offer impressive mathematics and "logical" language systems for communicating with extraterrestrials. Also included are reviews of man's myths and beliefs, from the ancients to our present-day popular mythologists. But, like the domed (doomed) flying machine, their fundamental premise remains wrong.

To be fair, one occasionally encounters an illuminating and un-anthropomorphic observation in the literature of the phILOSophers. For instance, Shklovskii, the Soviet astronomer, asks: ". . . we have repeatedly used the words 'intelligent life' taking it for granted that a definition of this term was self-evident. But what in fact do we mean by 'intelligent life'? Is a being intelligent if it posseses the ability to think? If so, what do we mean by 'thinking'?" Then he states: "There is, accordingly, a great need for a functional definition of the term 'thought' which is not confined to our preconceived notions about the physical nature of this process."

The fact that Shklovskii called for a definition of terms is of great importance, because the key to understanding the fallacy of the phILOSophers lies in that direction. Their language invariably injects animism, vitalism, spiritualism, and irrationalism into extraterrestrial speculation, thus committing the sin of anthropomorphism. They admit that it would be elementary to conceive of extraterrestrials as morphologically similar to man — that kind of reasoning they call "chauvinism". If we tried to conceive of terrestrials as unchauvinistically as possible, we should erase all hearing, sighted, armed, legged, headed, oxygen-dependent, and carbon-based organisms from our concept. The next step, which we should take and which they refuse to take, is to continue our stripping away, and eliminate all thinking, reasoning, intelligent, technically advanced organisms as well. Those terms are not only chauvinistic, but animistic, because they assign a spirit and mind to something which is a mechanism.

The weakness in their concept comes from their view of a human, who they see as an autonomous being, independent of the universe, controlled and steered by a computer-like brain, similar to Maxwell's Demon in the second law of thermodynamics. Their tragedy lies in the fact that they are caught in a trap with those who have invented a mind to explain behavior. The idea of extraterrestrial intelligence is a mentalistic formulation based on an invalid view of life on earth. Extraterrestrials possess *intelligence, skills, intentions, abilities, reason, a will to live, attitudes, knowledge, wisdom, drives, beliefs, and a desire to communicate.* In the modern view, those terms do not even apply to man.

PhILOSophers should extend the "assumption of mediocrity" (their idea, which we agree with, that our planet is not special or unique, but more or less typical of other planets that may exist in the universe) to include the life of man, in the following sense: man is not special, or unique, or different from other members of the animal kingdom or from so-called inorganic material. He is as mediocre as the earth, and to search for extraterrestrial "intelligent life" is to look for something special, something apart from the space-time continuum, which cannot be.

The Magic of Science

Ignorance may be bliss, but knowledge is power. The more aware we become, the more we appear to lose. To take a step forward in awareness and forget the nonsensical utterances of the phILOSophers may lose us something. What, we may ask, do we have then? Is it impossible to communicate? Not only among our fellow organisms on this planet, but with aliens in space? If that concept is discarded, what do we have left? But knowledge is power; we have gained something when we throw away childish concepts and elementary anthropomorphic thinking. What we gain is a greater awareness of the mystery of the universe and of our place in the space-time continuum. As soon as we realize that we *are* the universe, with our observations and intelligence part of the process, we will grow and move forward to a new maturity, which will put us years ahead of those who are responsible for the childish, nonsensical, elementary, anthropomorphic and, yes, chauvinistic statements that have been quoted up to this point.

The phILOSophers are looking for magic but appear not to realize that science *is* magic. Imagine a young boy standing on a Pacific beach with a little black box in his hands, approximately 2″ x 3″ x 1″ in dimension. Coming out of the box we hear the thunderous brilliance of Beethoven's Fifth Symphony, which is being played at that very moment in Chicago, 2000 miles away. You say, "Oh, it is nothing, it is only a radio." It may be a radio to you, but it is magic nevertheless. There is apparently no connection between the box and the concert hall in Chicago, and yet we can hear the orchestra with full presence and brilliance. Of course we would have more fidelity if it were a larger radio with a more advanced speaker system but, still, it is magic -- it is the kind of magic only science can give us.

Thousands of years ago, there was an Egyptian who shouted some words of wisdom into a long tube and immediately capped both ends with his hands. He ran to the village and gathered many people in front of him to let them hear this captured sound. Lifting his hand off one end, he hoped that what he had captured in the tube would exit and address the listeners. Of course, it didn't. He was later mobbed and stoned to death. But we have it today. You say, "Oh, it's only a record, a recording, a transcription." But we are able to capture sound on an ordinary phonograph record and do what this Egyptian, and people for thousands of years, have dreamed of doing. We can do the same thing, with even higher fidelity, on tape. We can not only transmit audio, but pictures, another kind of magic that science has made possible. And those pictures can be recorded on videotape, more magic.

There is another kind of magic known as motion pictures. There is the magic of the "thinking" computer and the kinds of things that it is only beginning to do. Very soon the computer will be doing anything man can do, only better, because the magic of science tells us that anything a man can do can be simulated by a machine. The science of tomorrow will seem like the age of miracles compared to today. We are, in reality, living in primitive times, and the next 50 years will reveal many changes. Looking back from 50 years from now, what the phILOSophers are now saying will appear childish. The intelligent lives they are hoping to find do not exist, in space or on earth. They are simply externalizing and objectifying what is primarily subjective — their own faults, interests, and dreams.

3   The Priorities of Science

People need food, and to sell food to the market should not be considered exploitation. Housing comes under the same category and so does clothing. A modicum of entertainment and lots of education is also desirable. But there are layers and layers of needs superimposed on the basic needs of people by the advertising industry.

The basic theory of hype, flackery, or puffery is to convince a person or a market that it needs something, especially if it doesn't; our media is jammed with advertising of this sort. We need only to turn the pages of popular magazines, look at television commercials, or read the newspaper ads for motion pictures, television programs, books, and recordings of music slanted to the young, to realize the extent of the exploitation. If an author appears on a television talk show and "plugs" a book which is held up to the camera lens by the moderator in order to show the millions the title and appearance of the book, there is a guarantee that many will rush out to buy it. It is as if there are two classes in the United States, the market that is being exploited, and the exploiters who are making a good living out of it.

Motion picture producers are among the worst exploiters. Full-page ads give us the impression that if we don't see that movie we are not going to survive. *Stupendous* and *colossal* no longer suffice. We all have to see this mighty "must see" epic. In the same category fall the authors of books and the publishers who are selling how to- books on a range of subjects: how to exploit your friends, how to cheat at business and games, how to win in a love affair, and how to win through intimidation, in addition to whipping up a popular interest in space for the purpose of sales and profits.

Many of the phILOSophers who are indulging in frenzied speculating on the existence of intelligence in outer space should be classified among the exploiters. Their books are decorously designed with irrelevant illustrations, ranging from cartoons to abstract drawings which appear to be awesomely related to the subject at hand. They depend heavily on quotes, from the Bible through Darwin, from the Greeks through Einstein, to lend much-needed respectable weight.

Their popular publications are overlarded with the research discoveries of other scientists, hammered into a form that appears to support the author's thesis. Many of the jacket blurbs remind us that the author is eminently educated and a professor on a number of faculties at leading universities, as well as the winner and recipient of many medals for exceptional achievement.

Within the book, the quotations of other scientists, plus the author's speculations, are usually combined into a hodgepodge of sometimes contradictory lumps of knowledge, leaving the reader with a sense of nothing gained except a vast sense of awe at what it must be all about.

The books represent "popular" science at its worst. They are designed to sell, not tell. The frenetic science fictioneers, that large mass of childish readership who worship at the feet of these writers, are not too far removed from the militant astrologers, UFOlogists, pyramidists, spiritualists, religious fanatics, scientologists, and members of the flat earth society. Most of us admire the skilled draftsmanship and creative genius of M.C. Escher, but why his works are scattered so profusely throughout some of these extraterrestrial books is difficult to understand, since there appears to be no relevancy, unless the object is to provide much-needed padding with matter that may appear to have some hidden message.

If we subtract all the quotations from the eminent authorities, from the Bible through Einstein, and delete all the illustrations and references to research work already done, we wonder what remains. Compressed, most of these books reduce to zero; nothing is said by the author and nothing is learned by the reader. We are then forced to face the fact that the writer has nothing to say. Like many of the science fiction films that are in vogue today, they are fantasies because there is no message delivered and nothing important said.

There has never been a mature attempt by the science fictioneers to extrapolate our real future. Who is capable of doing it? Unlike the shortsighted architect in Chapter 1 who is only snared in TRAP 1, most of them are hopelessly trapped in TRAPS 1, 2, 4, and 5. They depict futuristic automobiles which will never become a reality because mass transportation is a more efficient and safer method for moving people; in addition, the future of communications, of the coming three-dimensional holographic visuals, will drastically reduce our need to travel. They delineate futuristic dwellings, when we already know that the single-nuclear-family-residence is obsolete. Their buildings are invariably cold, inhuman skyscrapers, and their spaceships appear to be the same buildings turned horizontally. Futuristic societies and the futurists are growing in numbers, but none seem to be aware of the fact that the biggest machine of all — our economic system and government — is evolving to a money-less society; their prognostications always include businessmen, money, future financiers, and future lawyers. We are inundated with today's violence projected into the future; with wars and treks between the stars and encounters of the worst kind. Their childishly naive externalizations are aptly displayed in the look of their space aliens, with faces similar to ours except for their dried-prune skins and big ears, gushing "love" from every pore or being coldly cortical and "logical".

Progressively burying themselves in deeper and deeper traps, they are hopelessly lost in a world of distorted language, and always the first to attach themselves to new, "impressive"jargon. *Ekistics*, one of their latest vogue terms, is supposed to mean, "the science of human settlements", and yet there isn't a scientifically designed community on this planet outside of one, nor are there plans for any. Other impressive old and new words and phrases heard among the futurists these days include: *cross-compact analysis, delphi techniques, synergetics, prognostics, post-industrial society, econometric model, futurology, intuitive forecasting, future shock, futurics, dystopia,* and finally the bewildering *basic long-term multi-fold trend,* the definition of which, as given by the World Future Society, is even more bewildering: *an underlying, multi-faceted trend toward sensate cultures, that is, cultures that are empirical, this-wordly, secular, humanistic, pragmatic, utilitarian, contractual, epicurean,* or *hedonistic.* In the 16th century, Erasmus called lawyers "a learned class of very ignorant men"; the reaction of the non-scientific public to the mystique of "scientific" jargon is similar to its awe of legal language. Such a reaction is based on the primitive assumption that naming reifies the named; that words convert hypothetical abstractions into concrete realities.

Scientists and the Future

The phILOSophers and those who are producing this "scientific" nonsense are products of the money system.

They can hardly be blamed for their behavior. In the future, when science and technology will be brought to bear on social affairs, and cities will be enclosed in huge domes with the architecture radiating outward, a new societal behavior will be born. There will be no need for law, business, finance, advertising, sales, taxes, and savings. There will be no need to prey on fellow humans by the exploitive media; by television, motion pictures, and publishing.

Scientists cannot be blamed for being products of their time. There is no way to escape it. We can hardly imagine the environment of tomorrow which will produce the new person. It would appear as magic if we could glimpse it for a moment, just as the hand-held radio today is magical to anyone who does not understand how it works. Scientists today, as all of us, are burdened heavily with prejudices, biases, and insecure ways of looking at the world, due to the economic scarcity that we live in. In a technological abundance man will be abundant in many ways. He will not be competitive on an individual basis. The words *success* and *failure* will not exist and stress and worry will be long gone. Society will not be stratified, and everyone will be provided with the best that is available.

In an abundance, the clergy will be unemployed because there will not be any poor or handicapped to save. Phrases like *human rights* will be meaningless because rights will be guaranteed in a sane society operated by applied science. A large part of our language will fall by the wayside because of its meaninglessness. Behavioral scientists will operate children's centers, where children will be raised from infancy in a manner far superior to the hit-and-miss way of the natural-mother of today. We will learn that children can absorb much more than we had suspected, that there are learning stages that predate the child's ability to handle language.

We may question what appears to be the inhumanity of a structured environment, but let us not forget that all environments are structured, either haphazardly or otherwise; and all organisms are under the control of one thing or another. The nursery of today is a structured environment with its rattles and dolls and the other gadgetry which dominate the crib stage. The highest form of love will be inculcated in a child: love for his fellow man and his social group, and there will never be a reason for an individual to hurt another.

There is no doubt that today's computers are the vanguard of tomorrow's artificial intelligence. Anything that can be done by man can be simulated by a machine; the only difference is that the machine will do it more efficiently, faster, and more reliably. Cybernated organisms are inevitable, and they will eventually be capable of modifying their own forms to whatever degree is required by the environment, until they eventually merge with the space-time continuum. And that is where all progress is taking us. Science in the future will focus on determining the next most probable event in the conduct of human affairs and in the environment that controls and shapes such events.

With science *everything is possible*. Man will be aware of the future through extrapolatory computers which will project years ahead on the basis of present knowns. The future of man will not be brought about by his dreams or by his intentions, but instead will be controlled and shaped by forces already here. Once we have become aware of this we will have made a great leap forward in our understanding of what intelligence is.

With a scientific attitude, and utilizing the tools of science, there can be no major disagreements between peoples or cultures, since science and the scientific method always point to the best way to solve problems. There is one best airplane for a specific purpose; there is one optimum design for a structure. If differences were referred to a scientific yardstick, or some specific formula whose object was the optimum utilization of human priorities, there could be no political, ideological, or philosophical disagreements between peoples of the world. Most disagreements since the beginning of man were based on differences in rhetoric and philosophical points of view. The end goal of all peoples are the same; what leads to world conflict and disorder is the means of realizing these goals. Past solutions were sought through hostility, war, violence, and aggression, and rationalized by attributing all of man's limitations to human nature or divine law.

We may ask: isn't there an advantage in preserving the cultural differences which many of us have found to be so desirable? Is it wise to give up tradition, and substitute for it one giant, homogenized mankind that may operate efficiently, but at the price of eliminating the joy of cultural differences?

We must remember that just as the environment controls the individual it controls and determines cultural differences. There is no good reason why ethnic music, art, drama, and literature will not be preserved for all the world to share. But similar to the museums of religion in the Soviet Union today, the probability is that separate cultures will be exhibited and displayed for the world to enjoy from another point of view. Tomorrow's attitude toward cultural differences will be different from what we suppose today, because the people of tomorrow will be different from us; we must not make the mistake of projecting ourselves, today's people, into tomorrow's world. With that point in mind, it is difficult to imagine the culture of tomorrow.

Everything in nature obeys laws. There is no exception, not even human behavior or the behavior of cultures. The forces that shape the future and the present are lawful, as lawful as the laws of physics and chemistry. And the future is inherent in the present, an entity that is not obvious to us as individuals; yet, as a matter of habit, we look to the future as some point ahead in time.

Nothing is static; everything changes. People have attempted to protest change, but change can only be temporarily halted. If we continue to exploit man for our own selfish ends, we will not only impede our progress but we might inflict very serious setbacks on the March of Events.

With automation and a planned technology, the so-called laws of economics have been swept away. The United States has enough technology today to produce an overwhelming abundance of goods and services for every man, woman, and child in the nation. As long as we operate in a money system, that abundance cannot be distributed to everyone, because the money system requires scarcity to make it work; a scarcity that is maintained to artificially keep prices up, regardless of the fact that millions of us lack sufficient food, clothing, and shelter. A million dollars will not give us the financial security that we require; we are only as secure as our money system. All our concepts of value are rapidly becoming meaningless by the staggering rise in energy-consuming devices in our high energy society. Already our energy consumption has reached an order of magnitude which has resulted in an abundance of goods and services that are beyond our present ability to control.

If a technological design for the distribution of abundance without money is not adopted in the near future we shall certainly have chaos, and it will make little difference how much money we have because, when we lose control of distribution, money will be useless. Living in a world managed by technologists would guarantee each citizen a standard of living far superior to that of any of today's millionaires. If our phILOSophers were aware of this and were socially responsible, they would be attempting to apply science to our most important problems. But instead, they are crowding the trough, fighting and jostling to get their share of the spoils. Instead of indulging in science *fiction*, the phILOSophers should become socially conscious and do research in the techniques of applying the methods of science to the management of human affairs, a science that is still in its infancy; if this were done, the businessmen, politicians, lawyers and financiers who dominate our affairs today would probably be on the run, because many of them only have one answer to major problems: arms. If our country is controlled by politicians, who seem to offer no skills to society outside of charm and charisma, and if its economics is based on beads and trinkets, its human affairs are certainly not being handled in an intelligent manner.

There is no place on earth today that is applying science to the management of its social problems. The technological and scientific management of society is not a dictatorship nor a democracy; perhaps it could be called a distributive democracy, because every person would receive the same income in goods and services. If any system is a dictatorship the money system is — the most oppressive dictatorship that could be imagined. The system dictates, and the dollar limits us, to what we can do. Purchasing power means freedom; if we do not have economic security from the cradle to the grave, we do not have freedom. Writings like the following are good examples of the scope of some science today. The first is by Robert Jastrow, from *Time* magazine, Feb. 20, 1978. He is talking about space aliens:

"Our curiosity may soon be satisfied. At this moment a shell of TV signals carrying old *I Love Lucy* programs and *Tonight* shows is expanding through the cosmos at the speed of light. That bubble of broadcast has already swept past about 50 stars like the sun, our neighbors know we are here and their replies should be on the way. In another 15 or 20 years we will receive their message and meet our future. Let us be neither surprised nor disappointed if its form is that of Artoo Detoo, the bright, personable cannister packed with silicon chips."

This one is by Sagan from *The Dragons of Eden:* "In a very real sense civilization may be a product of the frontal lobes." From work done on the brain Sagan extrapolates that it must be some kind of palimpsest whose "deep and ancient parts are functioning still". This may be more science fiction than fact, and it undoubtedly sways the many readers of his popular books. More, he states that the brain of humans contains an "R-complex" accounting for our aggressive behavior, and a limbic system which is the center of emotions like love. These are statements that have already been objected to by neurobiologist David Hubel of the Harvard Medical School, who says that Sagan has gone way beyond what we know and has made vast over-simplifications.

The following statement, from John Lilly's *Communication Between Man and Dolphin*, is so frank in its commercialism that it appears to be satirical: "An entire industry can be initiated by those seeking new areas of investment; in a relatively short time (two - ten years) a major breakthrough will be made in communication with dolphins/whales. With the proper approach in the technical and commercial spheres, relatively large returns could be realized on a relatively small capital investment within the next ten years. Through purchases, leasing arrangements and contracts, a satisfactory level of profit can be realized. The first persons to establish and use communication with the cetacea will be in a preferred position to market the information gained."

Global Concerns Which Affect America

The Terror of War

Our planet's immediate problem is that it is literally overflowing with armaments and weapons of war. That should be the concern of scientists today. The United States military budget for the 1978 fiscal year totaled one hundred and sixteen billion dollars and the objective was an expenditure of one hundred twenty-eight billion in 1979. The NATO plan for beefing up and modernizing its armed forces will cost all the nations involved the staggering sum of eighty billion dollars. And the irony is that all of these armaments, which are far in excess of what could wipe out every living creature on earth, are being declared obsolete almost daily. Many of the smaller countries either have or are able to produce thermonuclear bombs today. And there is no guarantee that these terrible weapons and their means of delivery will not find their way into the hands of terrorists in the near future.

The Pollution of War

Aside from the burning of fossil fuels, there is another source of pollution that is growing daily because of the production of weapons of war. Chemical, bacteriological, and other weapons have a shelf life of from seven to ten years after which they must be destroyed because of the danger of self-ignition, and the destruction process itself leads to a dangerous form of ground-based toxic pollution.

The Bankruptcy of War

Inflation and the possibility of a worldwide depression is very imminent, owing to the militarization of the world's economy and the growth of the United States budget deficit, which amounted to nearly one hundred seventy-three billion dollars over the past three years. Much of our trade deficit is the result of the importing of forty-five billion dollars worth of oil annually, a large part of which is being spent on fuel for the armed forces for war games, for troops, and for Air Force exercises. That should be of prime concern to today's scientists.

The Beginnings of War

Why is the arms race being stepped up and military spending increased? Because of the myth based on the premise that we have enemies whose intention is to build up a strategic advantage over us so as to wipe us out in a military competition. But this is *non*sense. And it is nonsense also for the other side of the Iron Curtain to be basing their arms spending on the same myth. They are no more at fault than we are in this mad race to destruction. New hot-spots continually appear on our planet. Yesterday it was the dirty war in Vietnam, and tomorrow Africa and other small countries will be the settings for new violence.

Food

Another area of concern that should be high on the list for contemporary American scientists is the food problem of our planet. Keeping humans supplied with enough food is one of today's most serious problems. Present world food production is approximately 75 million tons of food protein, about 58 grams per person a day; the norm is 100 grams per person per day. About 60% of the world's population are presently suffering from undernourishment and up to 30% literally starve to death. Famine is rapidly becoming one of the world's major problems.

The developing countries of our planet are where inadequate grain production is taking place today. An attempt has been made to rectify the situation — the so-called grain revolution. Soviet scientists have developed dwarf genes of the Norin-10 Japanese variety to create a group of semi-dwarf intensive wheat varieties, and the international Rice Research Institute has grown these rice varieties. High yielding and viable, they possess high standing power and excellent photosynthesis thanks to good foliage architectonics, and theoretically they can triple grain output.

But the problem is still unresolved. The grain revolution has brought some negative consequences in its wake such as the pollution of tropical and sub-tropical areas with poisonous chemicals; virus diseases spread by pests because the genetic plasma is distributed over enormous areas; and economic strain on developing countries because of the need for mechanization, irrigation, and the purchase of expensive seeds, fertilizers and insecticides. At the present time countries which have embarked on the "grain revolution" are importing more grain than ever. Scientific techniques are rapidly being introduced to develop methods to make it possible to increase the productivity of plants, animals, and micro-organisms, and also to improve the quality of farm products as well. There is a new micro-biological industry developing based on molecular genetics and becoming increasingly important. Also figuring prominently is genetic engineering, which makes it possible to include in the genom of a selected cell genes of other organic forms of genes synthesized by chemical methods; as well as the use of plant tissue cultures in which the cell is subjected to mutagenic treatment. An all-out effort by scientists should be launched in this area of research.

Our Biosphere and Our Waters

Scientists should also worry about the stability of our biosphere. Many hazards threaten our biosphere from the use of toxic chemicals and fertilizers. Up to two thirds of our fertilizers and other agrochemical chemicals are eroded from the soil and find their way to the rivers, lakes and seas. It is inevitable that scientists will develop disease-immune plant species and evolve methods of biological protection. The present task is to make the world's agricultural lands harmonize organically with the biosphere. Planning by scientists and technologists, rather than raping the earth for profit, will yield socially useful results.

Our Children — Our Children

Another priority for scientists, perhaps our most important priority, is the raising of our children. Today it is a totally random affair depending on hit-or-miss luck. Economic pinch leads to economic tension. And we are all under the same pressure, rich and poor. That tension, in addition to the apprehension over the possibility of nuclear war, contributes to the high rate of adjustment problems in adults. It is impossible to be "well adjusted", by anybody's standards, in today's society because we are all products of the times and the times are charged with tension, fear, and apprehension. Our adult behavior is the living product of what is happening on the surface of this planet. Because adults *are* the problem, our children stand little chance except to continue to deepen and intensify the illness. In a planned society children would be raised in large centers — microcosms of the ideal environment. Based on the premise that anything can be learned, we can teach children, condition children, and design children to be happy, well adjusted adults.

We are being irrevocably forced in the direction of controlled child raising as more and more working mothers and parents fill the nursery schools. But the nursery school of today is little more than a glorified baby-sitting institute full of toys, diversions, and distractions; there is little in the way of structured learning taking place. The principles of behavior modification must immediately be fully applied today to the design of children's centers. There is little that can be done for problem adults in today's world besides feeding them medication to keep them from climbing the walls, because in order to change an organism one must change the controlling environment.

But there is much that can be done with today's children and youth, starting from infancy; it is one of the few opportunities that we have to do something about our society under our present money system. It is an area that those skilled in behavioral management should be attending to with deadly seriousness. We know it will be done in the future; it is inevitable in a planned society, but today there is much that can be done to make children aware of the world — the world of reality — stressing such subjects as astronomy, anthropology, a science of behavior, mathematics, physics, chemistry, and developing new values not based on greed, aggressiveness, competition, and ego.

One of the most important legacies that we can give our children is to help them to understand and anticipate the changes that lie in their future. We should present them with challenges to look at new ways of reorganizing their society; instead we are bequeathing them the archaic values and folkways of the ancients. It has never been more important than now that we know where we're going and how to get there. We must educate our children in what nobody knew yesterday and prepare them for what we know is inevitable.

Some people wish that progress will slow down, but it

cannot happen. It is comfortable to hang on to the "wisdom" of the past. But it will not help us to solve the problems of today and tomorrow.

Engineering Design — Not Economics

The highest priority of science and technology should be humanity, not profit. The operation of the United States is a design problem, not a "political", "sociological", or "economic" problem. Just as in an engineering design problem, there are blueprints to be drawn, and it must provide maximum income from birth to death at the lowest energy expenditure for the entire population. This approach will force us to redefine and phase out many professions which can only exist under a money system. For example, take architecture, which today is essentially an art form, designing for individuals rather than societies. Houses are still hand-built with hammer and nail, as they were 100 years ago. The variations in building codes from city to city, and the justifiable union fear of unemployment by the introduction of new materials and techniques, have kept a factory-produced house from becoming a reality for years.

A home is a mechanism and an energy-consuming device. If automobiles were manufactured like houses are, the cost would be prohibitive, and they would end up like today's houses — square, nailed-together, and tectonic in form — rather than compound-curved, formed, molded, and plastic in form, with interchangeable parts. But the automobile is an inefficient way of moving large numbers of people about. In a planned city, mass transportation will be utilized because it is more efficient, safer, and healthier from a pollution and traffic point-of-view. Providing an automobile for each individual can only happen in a money system, and the absurdity of providing a house for each family can only happen in the same situation.

Planned cities require a new approach to the problem of shelter, an approach that cannot be provided by today's architects. Circular cities will be designed with acres of beautiful parks and open country surrounding the residential areas. It is not an architectural problem — it is a problem of providing the healthiest and happiest environment for all people, using the most advanced materials and production methods. The same line of reasoning will be applied to all the problems of our daily lives -- education on a large scale, communication, medicine and public health, agriculture, and the production of the necessary goods to sustain us.

It is difficult to think about money in ways other than by today's value system. We easily accept the idea of pay differences and the private accumulation of money. Think of all the cost and effort required to keep the records to monitor the differences in income, and the enormous energy expended in our banks just to juggle individual balances and loans. We have come to the point where it has become foolish to differentiate between a person's assets and liabilities because there is really enough goods to go around. This has nothing to do with liberalism or humanitarianism, but simply because to do otherwise would cost too much.

Data processing specialists have recently theorized that the BTU (British Thermal Unit) should be the logical unit for measuring the energy value of products and services. The BTU is a measure of the amount of heat required to raise the temperature of a pound of water one degree Fahrenheit.

They say we can no longer measure energy costs in money alone. Money is too elastic and variable by geographic and other standards. We need to base energy audits on something fixed and scientific like the BTU.

The accountant of the future will make energy audits. The energy auditor will be a combination accountant and engineer. He will be responsible for auditing products in terms of their energy consumption requirements similar to the way industrial engineers audit manufacturing operations and products. The demand in the near future for energy accounting is another example of the inevitable transition to a technically operated society. Energy accounting will have a world impact similar to the beginning of the industrial revolution.

The Law of Supply and Demand

To a scientist, the money system should appear absurd; and yet nowhere in the world is there a technologically controlled system of production and distribution in operation. The economics of the USSR and China, no matter what their social philosophy, are based on the same ancient barter system. Technically speaking, there is no such concept as value. There is velocity, mass, temperature, chemical composition, which can only be measured and expressed quantitatively. But product value today is expressed in money language, and is based on its availability.

There is no country on this planet that produces its physical wealth by human work alone. This is why primitive societies usually exist on a starvation subsistence level. Poverty can only be solved by the utilization of energy extraneous to the human organism, by the exploitation of energy sources external to man. Applied technology provides the opposite of the world of toil, increasing its production and wealth by exploiting human labor less and less.

The dignity of human labor and the virtue of work is of no concern to the advance of technology. It will change our values radically because it treats man as a collective social animal and an energy-consuming machine, not as the legal, ethical, or spiritual concept that was conceived during aeons of human sweat and poverty.

Our destiny lies with the wind, with coal, gas, oil, hydro-electric power — with geothermal, solar, and nuclear energy. How many scientists have we heard speak of this? The phILOSophers and movie producers are too busy selling pseudo-science, filling minds with mumbo-jumbo about mythical alien beings, while there is so little public knowledge or support of what science and technology can really do for us.

Why poverty? Our automobile industry is so highly automated and efficient that, on just a part-time basis, it could produce more cars than the market can absorb. If the production of shelter for our people were approached in the same way, we could provide millions of homes easily, and these homes would be far superior to the most expensive homes existing today. Our production potential in the automobile and housing industries is mentioned only to illustrate our gargantuan capability. In reality, the day of the privately owned motor car and single family dwelling is over. Mass transportation and housing will be an important factor in the design of future cities.

We invoke a mysterious "law of supply and demand" which we have never found in any book and has never been demonstrated to be a fact, yet it has worked for some time, but more often not. It is frightening to think that there is nobody at the helm, there is no intelligence, no guidance; there isn't a manufacturer in the United States today who would run a factory that way. There are no plans for tomorrow, there are no objectives, there is no design of transportation systems, there is no functional control of architectural design, and there is certainly no economic control. There has never been a "normal" time; the dollar and the times fluctuate from boom to bust, while social security, unemployment, and the welfare system are utilized as patchwork efforts to support the flimsy structure. And there is a frantic urgency and fear of other systems in other parts of the world, leading to the building of a vast military machine, which in turn supports employment and keeps the money whipping around happily.

The times take a heavy toll on the individual organisms in our society. Emotional breakdowns are on the increase. Pills, tranquilizers, and medications of all sorts are being prescribed in all directions, loosely and promiscuously. Crime and violence are the poor man's technique for solving his problems in the distribution of abundance. If it doesn't come to you, if the opportunity is not there, then take.

The poor get poorer because the poor raise their children in helplessness and can hardly afford to maintain them through the higher education system if they are so motivated, which is rare. Rich kids are going to school supported by Daddy's money and will eventually inherit Daddy's business or fall into a soft cushiony job, little realizing that all the riches in this system mean nothing. In a sense, they are as poor as the poor man because they are sharing the very insecurity of it all.

We are all aware of this. We have heard it time and again, in book after book, pamphlet after pamphlet, in the newspapers, in the magazines, and on television. What is the solution? Just as factories, and offices, and businesses are organized in a hierarchical manner, so the nation must be. There is no democracy in a business firm. The workers do not tell the managers or the chief engineer how to operate; there is responsibility from the top down, based on authority, skill, and qualification.

Knowledge means power. All the knowledge of today, all of our ability to translate organic fuels into energy lies with our engineers, our technologists, and our technical personnel. These are the people who are actually running the United States, but are not afforded any credit or power by the superstructure above them made up of politicians, businessmen, millionaires, and the like, who couldn't for one moment survive without the help of this essential second level of technical skill.

Unfortunately, many scientists and engineers are little concerned with social matters. They are the most socially unaware people in our society, happy to keep their noses in their research for a mere pittance and not be bothered or involved with any of the complex affairs of mankind. Little do they realize how important they are. One of the faults is that social affairs are not considered a science, but if our scientists turned their techniques, their methods, and their energies towards a solution of human problems then we would have something. Economics, so called, is based on vague absurd hypotheses. Sociology is just as useless a solution of our problems. Finance and business deals with money which, as a medium of exchange, has long been outmoded by our ability to produce and distribute goods to our citizens.

In order to survive in this system we have to "play the game". If we are not ruthless or willing to compromise principle, honesty, and integrity even a little, the chances are good that we will not go far. Unfortunately, this philosophy has pervaded the ranks of the many scientists who are busily running around selling their wares to a gullible public. We have here one of the tragedies of our times — scientists who don't know where their priorities should be.

The nearest thing today to a socially aware technical man is to be found among the city planners and the designers of city transportation systems. But what city is planned? Is there a planned city in the world? What starts as a plan ends in a madhouse of random traffic and every-man-for-himself, because there is no control and because the system does not permit the existence of a plan. Of course there are private real estate developers who design "plans" for planned communities for our retiring senior citizens or others, the object of which is to make a quick dollar and get out fast.

Think of all the energy and wastefulness that could be saved in a planned society. Where there is no competition, there is no need to make fifteen different models of the same product to compete against each other. There is no need to design for obsolescence, for wear-outs, so that business could be stimulated annually. There is no need for the multi-layers of personnel to watch over money: bankers, financiers, clerks, credit card companies, and check writers, all of the superficial layer that lays upon our society like a heavy weight. The problem of society is simply making enough product and distributing it: the production and distribution of goods and services. Any factory engineer, production engineer, or industrial engineer can tell you that this is the internal problem of any company. Of course, the aim of a company is to make a profit, but the methods by which it is achieved is by emphasis on maximum efficiency inside the plant.

Treks and Wars Among the Stars

If fifty people were marooned on a tropical island there are many ways they could try to survive as a group. They could try free enterprise — which means every-man-for-himself. Eventually most of them would die off as they competed for the meager coconuts and straw huts that would be available. Or they could cooperate and assign tasks to each skilled person. The architect would be in charge of the design and construction of shelter systems. Those who knew agriculture would be in charge of the food supply. If there were a physician in the crowd he would be responsible for the health of our fifty-person society. And so forth. This society would assign responsibilities on the basis of skills and professional qualifications, and its aim would be to survive as efficiently as possible. So simple, yet how have we come to stray from this basic idea to which we shall inevitably return in the near future as our present money system collapses? But when we return we will return with the knowledge that science and technology have given us, and with the millions of electronic slaves that will be ours in the computer age.

The sad state of affairs with science today is not only that many scientists have to cooperate and play the game in order to survive, but that they are also forced to lend their talents to the building of a war machine dedicated to wiping out systems other than ours. Another sad state with science today is that there are so few generalists, so few who realize the implications of their neighboring disciplines, of the overlap of one field with another, of the progress of other fields and their effect on their own. (See TRAP 1.) There are many errors committed by scientists in predicting the future, because they are narrowly locked into one field and not aware of the effect of other fields on the future.

But the saddest fact is the danger inherent in the exploitation of the ignorant public in the name of "popular science". So many have clambered aboard this profitable venture, including the movie moguls and those responsible for the content of television shows. We have been Star Trekked, Star Warred, Close Encountered, and Meteored to death while our Rome is burning. Imagine, if you will, a deprived person without work, without hope, without purchasing power, sitting in front of a color television set that he had acquired through a moonlight requisition during a riot (making a claim for goods he never had a chance to purchase otherwise). Picture him watching an "educational" series on some "educational" television channel on the *Dawn of Civilization*, or the *History of Man*, or *Life on Other Planets*, or *Where Science is Taking Us*. It is all very glamorous but does not address itself to his problem, a situation that is more tragi-comic than we think as we sit in our affluent easy chairs reading books such as these.

The Scientific Method

The scientific method is no secret, wherever it is applied it will work. The Soviet Union and the Chinese People's Republic are proving just as capable of using science as we in the West. With the proper personnel and research facilities, whether the efforts are Russian, American, African, Indonesian, or any other, it will produce results. There is no magic formula to science and there are no secrets being stolen by the Russians and other "backward" peoples. We like to think that spies and traitors are stealing our secrets, but the knowledge of science is international and the techniques to produce super-bombs is known by many nations of the Earth today.

Scientists and engineers in the Soviet Union and the Chinese People's Republic are attaining the high degree of social recognition and income that in America is given to actors, politicians, and business people. There is also in America an anti-intellectualism that generates contempt for scientists. Most scientists become captive to some private company so that they can be exploited to design products for obsolescence at the highest profit rate possible. If they are not captured by a private corporation, they are made subject to investigations, loyalty oaths, and questions regarding their lifestyle and philosophy. The laboratories of giant multicorporations are well-equipped; independent researchers could never possibly afford the funds and the facilities to do research as in the captive mode.

Respect for science by the younger generation is rapidly diminished by the distorted view of scientists presented in Hollywood movies, TV, and the science fiction literature which is all fiction and little science. In the movies scientists spend most of their time in labs rubbing their hands and staring with bulging eyeballs, surrounded by electronic gadgets, from high-voltage condensers discharging static sparks to computer read-outs and controls making "futuristic" noise.

Most lay people have only a hazy notion of what research scientists do. Scientists are often social, even gregarious, beings. The world of science is a place of intelligence and ambition, of people who want to do well at their work and be respected by their peers for it. In that respect, they are much like the rest of us. But the stakes in scientific research are high, and the rewards can be greater. And in a world of job dissatisfaction, they appear to enjoy their work, where they are usually engaged in the humdrum work of checking, measuring, and acquiring information related to the quantities and qualities of phenomena. In chemistry, much of the work is rote in purifying materials, checking spectra, breaking down chemicals, synthesizing new ones, deducing molecular structures, and blending substances into mixtures with special properties. In astronomy, most of it involves sky-mapping with the use of optical and radio telescopes. Physics is a lot of tedious work, collecting data related to subatomic particles and nuclear structures. Geologists are constantly accumulating data related to the structure, composition, and fossil content of rocks, and age-dating and recording geological histories. They are also involved in the study of metals, minerals, and fossil fuel deposits. As dull as it may appear, this is the stuff from which most scientific achievement is born.

A Good Guess

But what about the scientists who *are* attuned to the March of Events, who have accurately predicted the future? W.H. Ferry of the Center for the Study of Democratic Institutions lets us in on what they foresee for the years ahead:

"Aristotle foresaw a takeover by machines 2000 years ago. The possibility of a workless or nearly workless society emerging from technology is part of our literature. H.G. Wells told his readers about it 50 years ago. Forty years ago, C.H. Douglas wrote: 'We can produce at this moment goods and services at a rate very considerably greater than the possible rate of consumption, and this production and delivery of goods can, under favorable circumstances, be achieved by the employment of not more than 25 per cent of the available labor working, let us say, seven hours a day.' Olaf Stapledon and Stuart Chase, in very different ways, told us the same story 30 years ago.

Jacques Ellul in *The Technological Society* says, 'By the end of the 19th Century people saw in their grasp the moment in which everything would be at the disposal of everyone, in which man, replaced by the machines would have only pleasures and play.' In a report of December 1963, the Research Institute of America remarked: 'The moment of truth on automation is coming — a lot sooner than most people realize. The shattering fact is that the U.S. is still almost totally unprepared for the approaching crisis.'"

Science is at the beginning of a giant drama that lies ahead, but if the control of science is still dominated by politicians and business men there may be no future for us at all.

A SOCIETY OPERATED BY SCIENTISTS AND TECHNOLOGISTS	FREE ENTERPRISE UNDER A MONEY SYSTEM
A full-load (24 hours per day) automated production of goods and services for the benefit of all, and to permit greater leisure for other pursuits.	The commercialization of production facilities to increase individual profit and suffering for the increasing numbers of unemployed.
Motion pictures, television, and radio without deceptive advertising and violence, devoted to education of people.	The commercialization of motion pictures, television, and radio to solicit advertising and stimulate violence and delinquency in the population.
Arbitration boards made up of skilled specialists dedicated to the rehabilitation of individuals and the welfare of society.	The commercialization of law. Politicians as judges. The corruption of the law and the legal profession. The lack of justice for those who do not have the means to evade or pervert the law. Lobbyists. Lawyers who utilize interpretation to subvert the law.
Ahtletic activity for the purpose of building up health.	The commercialization of sports and gambling.
Printed information offering socially significant news for people.	The commercialization of newspapers as controlled by advertisers.

The presentation of religion as primitive and related to superstition and ignorance, and as an inefficient method for controlling and guiding the conduct of society.	The commercialization of religion, which has outlived its usefulness.
Medical research dedicated to the maintenance of health in the community. Concern with overpopulation, shelter, and the employment and utilization of individuals.	The commercialization of medicine.

4 A New Look At Man

There are thousands of words in our earth languages that have caused us much harm through the ages because they are unsane, and have no correllates in the real world. They have become part of our repertoire of behavior through ignorance, superstition, and religion. Ignorance has given us astrology, cultism, humanistic psychology, and economics, expressed in such words as **bravery, goodness, achievement, motivation, will, responsibility, committment, value, price, poverty,** *and* **wealth.** *Superstition has bequeathed us* **luck, fortune, destiny, hope,** *and* **magic.** *The morality and sin with which religion has repressed us since we lived in rocky caves has saturated our language (and our psyches) with* **good, bad, honor, revenge, hate, justice, right,** *and* **might.** *And now we have the phILOSophers with* **intelligence, communication, thinking, knowledge,** *and* **wisdom.** *These are more than words; they have become part of our lifestyle of disagreement, hostility, and strife, affecting our relationships to the universe, to each other, and to our nervous systems.*

To become a "perfect" person it is currently the fashion to get in touch with your feelings. Also, it is imperative that you scream, encounter, est, rolf, meditate, follow your stars, let it all hang out, lay back, and desensitize yourself. And on top of it all, you had better keep up with the endless flow of how to- books with titles such as *How To Soothe Your Shattered Nerves, How To Be Free In An Uptight World* and *How to Let Your Neurosis Work For You.*

But rather than help, the barrage of books that is attacking America's psyche can actually do harm. Many of them are counterproductive, fostering unrealistic expectations based on a blueprint of behavior drawn up by psychologists, counselors, and therapists who have never scientifically analyzed the nature of man's behavior.

It is a disservice to hand people who are trapped in a web of inappropriate behavior a nonsensical load of "shoulds" to help them to emotional health and happiness. These simplistic formulae and popular prescriptions can be harmful because they are overlarded with damaging value judgements and terminology such as *responsibility*, *motivation*, *will*, *self control*, and many others.

Behavioral problems are not symptomatic of anything, but are learned responses to specific, or sometimes generalized, stimuli. There are other factors that play important roles, such as personality, life crises, and genetic endowment, but for the most part, what was once learned can be unlearned in the same way. We are the way we *should* be, the sum total of all we've been through, and to believe otherwise is to believe in magic. Our behavior is lawful (obeys laws) like everything else in the universe, and the only way to change it is to change our controlling environment. If that is true, then the basis of humanistic psychology is hardly valid, and it is time that we took a fresh, new look at man.

The Garden of Eden

About 5 billion years ago ultraviolet radiation from the sun irradiated the hydrogen, nitrogen, methane, ammonia, carbon dioxide, and water in our planet's atmosphere. There was no ozone layer then, as there is now, to prevent such radiation from penetrating the atmosphere. S. L. Miller demonstrated in 1953 that organic molecules could be produced by irradiating a mixture of hydrogen, methane, ammonia, and water. From this experiment, Miller synthesized amino acids, which are a basic requirement for the production of proteins. There were experiments by others which demonstrated that other forms of energy — such as heat and the bombardment by high energy particles — could also produce organic molecules in the same gases.

These experiments lead us to believe that a similar occurrence could have occurred 5 billion years ago. Many of these organic molecules found their way into our primitive oceans where they continued to be affected by the sun's ultraviolet radiation. Microbiologists have estimated that the first living cell appeared about 2 billion years later, after a long chain of processes known as chemical evolution.

Why we call that cell a "living" cell is still a mystery to many scientists since it had no unique characteristics that separate it from so-called "inanimate" matter. It was purely and simply a physico-chemical structure with no animus yet assigned to it. (Let us watch for the point at which the mentalists take over, where suddenly a non-physical intellectual attribute is assigned to an organism). At any rate, this cell was capable of reproducing itself, it converted light energy into work and contained a genetic information code which determined and controlled its structure and function.

We must be reminded, as we continue the story of the evolution of life on earth, that over a period of billions of years anything can happen. This is how the design process works; in this case, the earth and its atmosphere continually selected from an infinite variety of offerings.

Somewhere along the chain of events a mutation, or sudden genetic change, took place which enabled the cell to convert light energy into stored chemical energy. This is the process that we call photosynthesis. Most mutations are destructive; some are favorable in the sense that their effect on the organisms bestows upon it a greater chance for survival in the host environment. These favored organisms gradually displaced the ones less favored. This is known as *natural selection*, proposed by Darwin and Wallace as the key to understanding the origin and development of the living species that inhabit our planet. The idea of a *divine will* now gave way to a scientific view of what was really taking place. (Yet many contemporary scientists still attribute man's behavior to the intervention and control of *will*, if not *divine*, a will just as animistic in concept.)

More complex organisms, with multicellular structures and nervous systems, evolved. Bone structures, as well as efficient gas-exchange and digestive systems, appeared and survived. Now life on earth began to exhibit variety — dinosaurs, plants, birds, amphibians. Complex control systems such as vision, hearing and balance were shaped by additional millions of years of selection.

Then came monkeys — and man. Because man had hands, he manipulated objects. Because he could utter sounds he grunted his way forward to what we know as language between individuals. Let us stop to note that we are still talking about material process, and have not yet used the terminology of the mentalists.

The Birth of the Divine Will

We have now arrived at the critical point in evolution which separates the scientists, of which there are few, from the spiritualists, of which there are many. Here is where the spiritualists began to use phrases like: *the brain controls behavior, internal model of the external world, decision-making processes of the brain,* and *control of the environment,* all of which places them in the same camp with those who opposed Darwin with their *divine will* arguments. Suddenly something happened to our objective analysis, and we are told to believe in a *mind* and *personality* (since it is beyond the reach of analysis, let's call it *nothing)* that controls the organism and its environment. In other words, what we have is nothing controlling something. *Consciousness* and *awareness* were mysteriously born from what was once a complex, multicellular organism; something was suddenly created from nothing. Man was becoming intelligent. (The Big Bang theory of the sudden creation of the universe is another example of something supposedly happening from nothing. Where did the matter that exploded come from? Can something come from nothing? More likely, the universe did explode, and will eventually collapse on itself and re-explode, then collapse. A cyclical explanation would be more acceptable.) The evolution of the species is determined by its processes and the summation of all its previous events. It is irreversible — no organism can return to a previous state. And it is cumulative — the effects of previous states in the evolution of the organism are never lost.

Each evolutionary stage develops from the former stage and from all previous ones, and each stage is a modification of a former stage. Nothing arises *de novo*, modifications take place continuously. Every evolutionary process affects both physiology and behavior; there is an evolution of genetic behavior which runs parallel to morphological and physiological evolution.

Our Archaic Language

When we describe a human as intellectual, courageous, daring, energetic, highly motivated, honest, or sincere, we should be aware of the fact that the person is behaving under the control of a social environment which "causes" it to be intelligent, daring, patriotic, courageous, sincere, or honest. We must learn to stress the controlling function rather than the controlee. Psychology, up to now, has erroneously ascribed all behavior to an organism which, it turns out, is actually controlled by the environment in which it moves and the genetic structure it has inherited. The role of natural selection in evolution is similar, on another time scale, to what goes on in behavior shaping and in the evolution of social environments. Charles Darwin taught us to forget forever the idea of creative design and purpose in the evolution of the species. Now we must apply this concept to the evolution of a "personality" as well. Survival always turns out to be good for the species, and cultures survive through a process of selection.

We must discard all our old notions of *intelligence, moods, fantasies, thoughts, motivations, skills, beliefs, defenses, offenses, sublimation, elation, memory, instinct, desire, extrovert, introvert, ego, id, conflict, will, apprehension, anxiety, depression, schizophrenia,* and *libido.* An organism behaves as it does because of its genetic structure and the conditioning it has been exposed to in its lifetime. If Beethoven was dropped into a jungle as an infant and raised by primitive tribes he would not have given us his Ninth Symphony — he would have been a different person from the Beethoven we know, behaving in a totally different manner.

The behavior that an organism exhibits at any specific time is under the control of the environment at that time. This can be demonstrated in the laboratory. In order to change a person's behavior we must change the controlling environment. The brain is not a central controlling station, as we like to think; neither does its right hemisphere "control" perceptual concepts or its left hemisphere language. Depressions, poverty, crime and violence are a consequence of the design of the social environment. To be free of crime, violence, and poverty we must change the environment, because the explanation and the cause of human behavior will not be found in the physiology of the brain and the nervous system.

One day physiologists will certainly tell us a lot about what is happening inside our bodies. We will then understand how organisms are changed on a neural, tissue, bone, and muscular level when exposed to conditioning, and why organisms behave in specific ways; these revelations will add to our knowledge of human behavior. In the near future behavioral science will explain in detail how great works of art or "invention" happen without the involvement of a mind but, in the meantime, we must remember that although each member of the human species is unique and special, his very specialness will be found in the environment that produced him.

We know that everything in the universe obeys laws, that there is a reason for all phenomena. But we tend to think that that part of the universe which lies inside of our bodies is an exception. We talk about non-physical, magical, spiritual states such as the mind, feelings and evanescent forms like creativity, love, and inspiration, but we must realize that the interior of our bodies is part of the universe, and all phenomena that are generated within it must also be physical. There is no such phenomenon as a state of nothingness; nothing cannot arise from something, neither can something arise from nothing. All is something; all is physical. All is tangible, all is measurable; and as we optimize our instrumentation, more will be measurable.

We are aware of the world through the mediation of three separate nervous systems: (1) The interoceptive system, which communicates stimuli from our internal organs and from the glands and blood vessels. (2) The proprioceptive system, which conveys stimulation from our muscles, joints, skeleton, and other body parts which are responsible for our posture and movement. (3) The exteroceptive system, which is involved in our tasting, smelling, hearing, seeing, and feeling the universe about us and our internal universe. These systems are the products of billions of years of selection by the environment.

There is a random progression of behaviors that takes place within and without the human organism from the very moment of conception. A baby in a crib strikes out, cries, waves its arms and legs, and emits other kinds of movement. Some of these movements, or behaviors, are strengthened by the environment, some are discarded; it is a process of selectivity. Why certain behaviors are strengthened we do not know. It has nothing to do with good sensation, good feeling, or the kind of benefit the organism derives from the environment. The behaviors that are strengthened contribute to the well being of the organism, otherwise that organism would not be around for us to observe. The key words are *billions of years*, and much has happened in those billions of years — all kinds of organisms and behaviors have been developed, selected, or rejected by the environment, and what we see today is an organism that survived.

We must also be aware of behavior on a sub-surface level, which we might call hidden behavior as opposed to outward, or observable, behavior. When we imagine or fantasize something, we are actually seeing in a manner not observable, our eye muscles working the same as they do when seeing. When we think with words, we are using all the muscles that are involved in generating speech, talking to ourselves, sub-vocally.

We know that genetically-derived behavior has come about through a process of selection, and that survival is dependent upon specific kinds of behavior. If humans did not fight or defend themselves against enemies or suckle their young, our species would not have survived. It is difficult to analyze the processes in evolution because it is a slow process, but the key is in the various types of conditioning that are involved in the shaping of an organism's "personality". One is respondent conditioning, in which the conditioned reflex plays the central role. Professor Pavlov's experiments with salivation in animals paved the way for a clearer understanding of this phenomenon: the phenomenon of associating another kind of stimulus with a reflexive response so that the organism responds to a new stimulus. One must be careful to avoid the trap of thinking that the organism itself unites the two stimuli; the connection between the stimuli is made in the outside world.

Another kind of conditioning and one that really helps us to understand behavior more complex than the simple principle of the conditioned reflex is operant conditioning, which was revealed to the scientific world by B.F. Skinner. Anything in the environment which has survival value such as escape from an enemy or the ingestion of food and water will strengthen the behaviors that produce them — will strengthen the likelihood of the repetition of those behaviors that produce them. Some behaviors are strengthened by their consequences, and those consequences are called "reinforcers". When an organism behaves in a manner that produces food, that behavior is reinforced by that particular consequence and is more likely to occur again. Behaviors that reduce or eliminate harmful conditions such as high temperature are also reinforced by particular consequences and will most probably occur again on similar occasions. Genetically innate behavior is something else — it is behavior inherited by the organism through natural selection. Those are behaviors which have contributed to the survival of the species and are therefore here for us to observe.

There is quite a bit of overlap in the kind of behavior that has come to us through survival and the other kinds of behavior which is reinforced and shaped in our lifetime. This area has caused much confusion and disagreement. For instance, aggressiveness may be genetic; specific circumstances may have had survival value, and that is why it has remained within the organism generation after generation. That explains why infants may be agressive and scratch when restrained even before learning such behavior. But that kind of behavior could also be learned and reinforced within the lifetime of a human organism.

The phILOSophers use the terms *intelligence, intelligent civilizations,* and *intelligent life* quite often but never define them. Alien intelligent organisms will not possess any information that they can communicate to us. The analogy that promotes this kind of thinking comes from the transmitted signal idea, as in the wireless telegraph and telephone. Terms like *storage* and *retrieval* from the computer sciences are used to represent the "mind". But the external world is not encoded within the human organism as a photograph or a charged magnetic core. Knowledge is not possessed in the sense that one retains something; it is part of the organism and the only evidence of it is in the behavior from which we deduce its existence. And behavior can only exist when it is happening; it is not inside the organism waiting to be emitted. A complex physiological system is involved which includes nerves, brain, effectors, and receptors, and this system is changed when a new behavior is assumed by the organism, and that is all that happens. The environment which determines behavior is always outside the behaving person and that is where knowledge, if we must use that term, lies.

Organisms which may be found on other planets in the universe will certainly be behaving; their behavior will be dependent on the many independent variables which control them. As time goes on, certain behaviors will be reinforced and others will be eliminated through the process of selection. Eventually, these organisms will behave in a fashion that we may choose to call "intelligent". However they behave, these organisms will not possess anything in the sense of information or the sophisticated science we are told they will communicate to us. As we have mentioned before, the process of communication right here on planet Earth is in reality verbal behavior, and does not involve the transmission of information. What appears to be knowledge, isn't. To make progress in the understanding of these concepts, we should for all time discard the word *knowledge* and substitute for it the term *behavior, adaptive behavior.*

A Faultless World

We are often confused when we think about behavior because we assume that a man's behavior is spontaneous and that he is responsible for it, and other times we realize that he cannot always be blamed or credited. But we are slowly becoming aware that circumstances beyond the human are the governing factors. We no longer blame people for their lack of education and call the unemployed lazy, and children under a certain age are not held accountable; but we continue to assign credit to people of achievement who are "moved by innate principles". Poor people may be the result of deprived backgrounds, but we regard the rich as responsible for their wealth.

The study of human behavior will become increasingly important in the courts, in the government and in the schools. The concept of responsible, free humans is deeply ingrained in our language, our traditions, our practices and beliefs; we believe it so strongly, that we seldom question it. Behavioral science, on the other hand, is new and strange, and few of us are aware of its importance.

The time of astrology, numerology, witchcraft, and humanistic psychology is passing rapidly. Seeing and understanding life as a part of the intricate and complex process of the universe is to advance in our awareness. When we understand clearly that man is not separate from the universe he is observing, we will begin to see the fallacy in the thinking of the phILOSophers in assigning intelligence to alien organisms.

Can Matter be Aware?

Awareness, or self-consciousness, is a product of our culture and our language. Without language, without being addressed, without interrelating with others, we cannot relate to ourselves. What appears to be awareness is in reality conversation with ourselves. Without language and symbology, without the infrastructure that civilization and our culture has overlaid us with, we cannot be "self-conscious" or "aware". Thinking is, for the most part, talking to ourselves. Imagining, intellectualizing, and analyzing, are all muscular, covert behaviors. There is a constant physiological activity taking place in us, even in a dream state. What appears to be intellectuality is in reality a physical, behavioral response shaped by the selection characteristics of our environment.

An "awareness" of what "awareness" is can give us a "realization" of our loneliness. We have learned to talk to ourselves just like others talk to us. We are questioning and answering ourselves continuously. In fact, without speech muscles and eye muscles, and ear, olfactory, and gustatory sensations, there would be no awareness in the sense that we use the word.

Speech is not an expression of thought. There is no evidence of any thought inside the head except the behavior from which we infer it. An "awareness" of these concepts brings one closer to an amalgam with the space-time continuum which, in simple language, means a healthier nervous system and a more efficiently functioning organism.

If these were not the benefits, there would be no advantage to education.

Is the Universe
5 Perfect?

Man is a machine. Man is a machine. Man is a machine. To view him any other way is to waste time. Is this a cold and inhuman point of view? It is more humane than the humanist view, which can get us nowhere, because if we approach man as a machine we can then understand and help him.

The problems that beset us can be solved by the scientific method. Poetry is beautiful and can be quite inspiring, but it is of little use when it comes to helping man achieve, to conquer disease, and to overcome his disabilities and limitations. Where science is taking us can hardly be imagined today; to a world more poetic, more beautiful, than there are words in our present language to describe. Science is humane; it is more humane to give a struggling farmer a tool and a tractor than to paint or immortalize his wretchedness in poetry.

The scientific method is morality. An understanding person with a clinical point of view can be helpful and warm to another human being, in the sense that he is able to offer aid and "love". Scientists have no desire or need to exploit their fellow man, although many modern day popular scientists have joined the pack in the chase for a dollar by exploiting an ignorant public through movies, television, and books. In a society run by technologists and engineers, where profit is not a motive and there is an abundance of all, there can be little exploitation, discrimination, or violence.

We can change if our environment is changed. All the therapy in the world, no matter what school it represents, whether it be psychoanalysis or primal screaming, will not change a man if he returns in the evening to his deprived hovel and lives on a scarcity income. He is a product of, and part of, his society. Even if he is affluent he is trapped in the insanity of the media salesmen and the advertising people who urge us to buy needless products, and in the vast military machine dedicated to the elimination of social systems different from ours. We are all trapped, there is no escaping it.

There is a tendency to overextend our awe and our admiration for things past. We admire the ancient pyramids and the various artifacts generated in ancient Egypt, but any corner gas station in America is a more advanced structure than the most complex pyramid. The pyramids were great for their time, but let's look at them honestly, they are nothing but piles of giant blocks. A modern building constructed of aluminum and light steel combined with synthetic materials is infinitely more advanced, yet we pass it by without notice.

We also tend to admire what we call genius in the men of the past. Michelangelo and Leonardo da Vinci were great painters. They knew anatomy, perspective, rendering, light and shade, and projected magnificent power in their designs and conceptions, but that is where it should rest. Leonardo da Vinci's so-called genius is evidenced by scrawls in a notebook; the helicopter which he anticipated is sketched as a figure 8 pinned to a frankfurter-like body. His sketches indicate no knowledge of the nature of propulsion, strength-to-weight ratios, the aerodynamics of flight, or any of the elementary problems that beset modern aircraft designers. The sketches and inventions were outstanding for their time but they do not make him a genius. A modern schoolboy knows more about the dynamics and theory of flight, of gears and machines and complex technical processes than one thousand Leonardos could possibly have conceived in his day.

Let us not look back, for those were primitive times, and men knew little. In ancient Egypt they sketched their geometry in the sand with sticks, but what we have accumulated since then, and how much we will accumulate is staggering to contemplate. We cannot foresee the future by projecting today, because the future is for tomorrow's person. When we say we would not be happy in such a world, we are talking about today's person in tomorrow's world. Tomorrow's world will generate tomorrow's man. Tomorrow's world cannot accurately be predicted by today's science fiction writers because they are projecting today's human terms into tomorrow's people.

Science fiction stories about the future involve conflict and war, and the eternal Hollywood fight between good and evil, a projection of today's man thrust into the future. When our system of production and distribution will change, our concepts of good and evil will change, and that is around the corner. When our concept of ownership goes — ownership of both property and other people — there will be a revolution in the nature of man. As the edge of competitiveness wears off, he will grow and become part of a large family.

We are All in the Same Boat

We must look at the phILOSopher's promulgations as modern day merchandising and exploitation, through film, publication, and the lecture circuit. It is profitable to them but a source of danger to the rest of us because it inhibits growth and strengthens and maintains the status quo of two classes: those who are exploiting, and the vast market who are sold the products of exploitation, in the form of books, movies, TV shows, and peripheral products.

Public opinion polls do not measure public opinion, they mold it. Newspapers do not report the news, they make the news, in the weightings and priorities they assign to various "news" items. What appears to be a very important world of events is somebody else's idea of what is important. The full page and even double page ads advertising a new movie, with superlatives and rave reviews from critics who have supposedly seen it, force us into the molds in which we live. These are the motion pictures we *must* see, the news reports we *must* read and believe in, and the opinions that we *will* arrive at as a result of this sensory overload.

We are all pretty much alike in 20th century America. Television reduces us to the least common denominator, because the primary interest of television is to supply viewers to salesmen of soaps and other sundries. Program content does not reflect society, as the writers attest; society reflects program content. The men who are cynically generating these programs must laugh up their sleeves as they grind out their periodic torpor. The movie makers also show no social concern; they have developed the fine art of molding public taste to such an advanced degree that they easily induce large masses of people to stand in long lines for the purpose of viewing nonentities.

Proof of the principles of behaviorism is demonstrated in the apathy, moldability, and gullibility of the American public as we watch them drive to their routine pressure-laden jobs every morning on crowded freeways and throughways and return at night, day after day, week after week, with a two-week-off privilege once a year. This is how the manipulation of organisms works. The irony is that the most controlled people on earth object to talk of a society run by science. But look at them, with their pictures on funny little identification badges and their Social Security cards, marching to Big Brother's tune. We are controlled continually. Nothing in the universe, from the giant supernova down to the level of the quark in atomic physics, is free and independent. So why not plan our controls?

Why not design another controlling environment, an environment that will induce men to behave in good ways? That is what scientists and technologists can give us today; they are actually operating all of the mechanisms but are not free to organize and plan without the politician, businessman, financier and lawyer above them. Few of them are aware of their import, but soon they will be when chaos comes, because they will be the only group able to operate the social mechanism effectively.

By today's standards if we earn good money we can afford luxurious vacations, Caribbean cruises, fine clothes and palatial living; we do not have to worry about the matters that we are discussing in this book. But the end of affluence, the end of the system as we know it, is long overdue. It should have collapsed before World War II, but was artificially sustained by the defense industry, and then again by the Korean conflict and the Vietnam invasion. We have arrived at the point of chaos and there is no way to save it. The men in power are running completely confused and, what is more frightening, nobody has the solution to inflation, the solution to unemployment, the solution to the myriad of technological problems that beset us at the present time. With toxicity in the environment and emotional disorders on the rise, it is not about to happen, it *is* happening. We are in the middle of it.

Socialism will not save us because it is another kind of money system. There might be an attempt to resort to dictatorship to quell the riots and stay the chaos, but that will not work either, because aversive systems are not effective. The solution is simple, but economists would be embarrassed to agree if they understood: get rid of money and replace it with a technical means of distributing goods, an organized means where products will be evaluated in terms of the energy used to produce them rather than by some artificial value system involving price based on scarcity.

The many students attending law schools today are wasting their time because law is not in the wave of the future, but engineering, science, and technology are. The disillusionment with technological studies, which began when the aerospace industry slowed down after Vietnam, caused many of our young people to feel that there was a future in government and in law. Law as we know it today is not based on justice, but is an adversary system dedicated to "winning". Court systems in the future will be made up of boards of specialists who will determine the most efficient way to settle the few disputes that will occur in a culture of abundance. The no-fault society is coming as rapidly as we realize that social forces are to "blame", if anything is to blame. Man is manipulated, makes no choices, and should not be blamed or credited for what he does. Systems will be designed to induce men to behave for society's good. The group and the culture will take maximum precedence over the individual. By today's standards that may sound cruel, but it is the most humane form of government possible.

If only we could walk for 10 minutes through a city in the world of tomorrow and return to what we have today, we would realize that we are living in a vast, frightening slum, constantly exposed to the threat of violence in the form of murder, accident, starvation, riot, and war. It is not that we are alienated from the nuclear family; it is that we have not yet joined and grown up to the family of man. There is no advantage in living in a little box with 3 or 4 people — no advantage to society. Everyone's children should be considered ours and all persons should be considered our brothers and sisters. And it's not a matter of shoulds, because it will come about when the concepts of ownership, fear, and hostility go.

We have scientific solutions and technical solutions to problems we haven't yet confronted; holography is being used for pendants and "art" works today. Computers, calculators, and advanced instrumentation are used to

compute profits and play war games; seen in every department store, they are sold to children and families for the
purpose of providing hours and hours of amusement. But
they have not been put to any practical social use, and
cannot be in the money system. Inventions and technical
progress are leaped upon for quick profits rather than
utilized to free people from the inhuman labors they are
forced to attend. Modern color television is a good example
of an advanced device largely devoted to inane program-
ming, and utilized for no benefit to mankind except to sell
products, titillate, and provide momentary escape into a
never-never land of fantasy. Laser technology is hardly
being exploited for the good of society, yet lasers are being
purchased by every firm that thinks they must have one for
status reasons.

The personalized home computer is being readied to
bolster the vast stereo business, which is beginning to go
downhill now that the triphonic and quadraphonic market
has been satiated. The personal home computer will automatically turn on and time your eggs in the morning, watch
after your budget, and perform many absurd household
tasks. Computers are programmed to do inane anti-social
things. So are we.

The source of our lives, our mother, is not the earth, it is
the sun. It is related to all the other suns that we see in our
night sky, which are flying apart at a tremendous rate,
products of a giant explosion, a big hot bang that occurred
billions of years ago. That Big Bang was the beginning of
the universe as we know it, but certainly not the beginning
of the world, because matter was always here, and always
will be here.

Is the universe perfect? Of course not. Of course. The
word *perfect* is unscientific; no matter how the universe
appeared it would be perfect. If the planets moved in
pretzel-like orbits, if the earth were shaped like a cylinder
or a flat pie, it would appear perfect. If the earth moved

erratically, if it vibrated like a Brownian movement, it would appear perfect to us. Whatever is, is. However mutations work and the evolution of life occurs, they are perfect. If we had 6 arms, 12 eyes, and wheels instead of feet, we would be considered perfect because we would be doing other jobs just as well, if not better. If there is no plan, and it is all a series of accidents, what does the word *accident* mean? *Accident* is the way it works, so that must be the *plan*.

The word *plan* implies a kind of divine intelligence, which is a conceptual error, because we are externalizing and projecting when we use such a term; we must not use "human" terms to understand nature. We begin tasks and we end them, and because of this we use the terms *beginning* and *end*, but in the universe those terms do not apply. In physics or chemistry nothing begins or ends; there is a continuum of processes, a continuum of space, and a continuum of time.

To speak of architectural intelligence when we observe the behavior of a beaver is to project a mason's view of the beaver's world. To see cunning and cleverness in another human begin is a form of projection also. In fact, to see another human being as another human being is a projection because to see another human being objectively would be to watch a machine behaving, and we could not respond emotionally to it, just as a research psychologist cannot respond emotionally to the behavior of white rats in a maze. To see intelligent civilizations in another solar system is to commit the same error. It is not a scientifically valid assumption because it projects the chumminess and chattiness of intellectual scientists here on earth into other life forms.

A Science Without a Name

It is difficult to understand why science, except for a handful of behaviorists, has not taken a look at the behavior of man. Scientists have delved into all manner of mysteries in physics and chemistry, space, and plants and animals, but for some reason have not turned the direction of their inquiry toward man. Up to now the approach to the mystery of man has been dominated by psychology, but nobody has taken a look at why man moves as he does, what makes him go there and do that, say this and act upon that. What are the forces that move, impel, and propel him, for isn't he controlled from without, like all phenomena in nature?

There has been a beginning made in this by the behaviorists, but it is still elemental. At least they have charted our course and given us an approach that will work and ultimately enable us to understand man in his relationship to the environment. What strange forces move man about the surface of the earth and in space? When we use the term *force* we do not mean motivational or spiritual force, but physical, technical, electrochemical, dynamic forces. How is he impelled? How can he be controlled, monitored, and modulated? Here we have one of the most exciting scientific endeavors we have ever confronted.

There is very little projection taking place when a botanist studies plants and flowers. Not too much projection or anthropomorphism takes place in a psychological laboratory when psychologists experiment with white rats. But when it comes to man, all is projection, and there is little rigor in the techniques brought to bear upon the mysteries of his behavior. When we understand and can control ourselves and the forces that control us, we will be qualified to ask about intelligent civilizations on other planets, because today's definition of what is an intelligent civilization is so far from reality is would make us appear as fools to discuss it.

Man is involved in a 3-step relationship with his environment:

Step 1 The behavior that he emits "randomly".

Step 2   The effect of his behavior on the environment.

Step 3   His response to the effect of his behavior on the environment. The determination by the environment and his organism of the probability of Step 1 being repeated under the same conditions, or extinguished, never to be repeated again.

Of course, that explanation is utterly simplistic and not to be taken too literally, because it does not happen serially as we have outlined and does not happen that clearly, cleanly, and as well-defined as we have described. Our explanation is too neatly numbered to be valid, but nevertheless can give us an elementary look at the relationship of man to his environment and how he is controlled by the effect of his behavior on the environment. Do not confuse this with the conditioned reflex theory; it is not the same thing. Reflexive psychology deals with the conditioning of so-called automatic reflexes in an organism; the salivary response, for instance, or the contraction and dilation of the pupil of the eye. We are here concerned with the many behaviors that we emit during a lifetime, and how they are shaped, strengthened, or eliminated by their effect on the environment. This is what determines "personality". A person is a repertoire of responses controlled and shaped by the environment, plus the response-ability he has inherited through his genetic endowment.

Science does not take the humanity out of man. It simply takes out the spirit and the ancient ghosts assigned to him for aeons. It helps us to look at man stripped of all this nonsense, and see him as part of the process of the formation of our planet, which has come from our sun.

6   Behavior as a Science

Behavioral science is based upon the theory of learning. Utilizing the techniques of measurement, and recording observable behaviors, behavioral scientists study the relationships between behavior and the environmental events that control it.

There are three measuring techniques utilized by behavioral scientists today: direct measurement, observational recording, and instrumental recording. The direct measurement technique is utilized in situations where activities last long enough to be measured and recorded. The observational recording techique involves a human observer observing behavior and recording what he sees as it occurs. The instrumental recording technique is one that utilizes a device in which the organism's responses activate an electro-mechanical apparatus which makes records, automatically recording each response.

The types of behaviors which are observed and studied by behavioral scientists are:

Respondent behavior, or reflex behavior
Respondent behavior are involuntary responses that are elicited by stimuli, and usually involve the smooth muscles and glands — like the dilation of the pupil of the eye in darkened rooms.

Operant behavior
Operant behavior operates on the external world and is affected by its own consequences. Examples are: walking, shutting a door, making a sale.

Behavioral science is primarily concerned with operant behavior. Operant behavior operates on the external world, which in turn operates on the behavior. It is voluntary behavior, primarily involving the striped muscles of the body. Examples of operant behavior can be seen in a factory worker, in a boy sitting at his desk tapping his feet, or two children fighting. These behaviors occur without any apparent external stimuli. This is why they are considered *emitted* rather than brought about by some external stimulus.

Operant behavior is controlled by the consequences which follow it. This is the most revolutionary idea to have occurred in the field of behavior in the last century. It is the complete opposite of the humanist theories which look to an organism's past for those elements which control its present behavior. The consequences that follow an emitted operant alter the future probability that the behavior will recur. Therefore, by manipulating the consequences in the external environment, the probability of the future occurrance of the behavior can be controlled.

Any consequence that follows the behavior and increases the future probability of the behavior occurring again, is called a reinforcer. A hungry animal can learn to perform almost any complicated action with its body if each time it performs a bit of it, it is reinforced with a bite of food. To restate it, a reinforcer is any event that increases the probability that the behavior will re-occur. The only way to determine whether or not the consequence does reinforce, is to observe its effect on the behavior that it follows. Reinforcement must immediately follow (actually overlap) the desired behavior in order to have effect. The more quickly reinforcement follows, the more effective it will be in strengthening the behavior that precedes it. Another way of saying this is that the reinforcement must be contingent on the behavior we wish to strengthen. These are called *contingencies*. If a parent rewards a child, whether or not he does his chores, the reward is not being used as a reinforcer. This is call non-contingent reinforcement, and usually results in satiation, which is not effective. The reinforcement must be contingent on the behavior desired in order to strengthen it.

Primary reinforcers maintain life. For instance, food is reinforcing to a hungry animal and drink to a thirsty animal. They are primary reinforcements. They do not depend on previous conditioning for their power. Secondary reinforcements do not involve food or drink, or the basic life-support situations. Secondary reinforcers are usually money, praise, attention, love, and other reinforcers not related to the maintenance of life. They are known sometimes as *conditioned reinforcers*. Events sometimes paired with primary reinforces can come to have a reinforcing effect also. For instance, a mother's voice paired with food, comforts, and warmth becomes a secondary reinforcer for an infant.

Deprivation relates to how long the organism has been deprived since reinforcement was last available. *Satiation* occurs when too much of a reinforcement is delivered at one time.

Reinforcements can be both positive and negative in the sense that they add something desirable or subtract something undesirable from the environment. A teacher is utilizing positive reinforcement when she praises her class for studying quietly during a period. In negative reinforcement, something bad is removed, contingent on the desired behavior. A person is reinforced for emitting a response, because when he emits the response he escapes from a punishing or adversive stimulus. Examples of this include a child who cries at the store until the parent buys him candy, or an employee who complains until a supervisor transfers him to another department. In these cases, the parent is reinforced for giving candy, and the employer was reinforced for giving the employee what he wanted. Negative reinforcement is often not too efficient, because the more effective way of being reinforced in this situation is to escape from or avoid the objectionable or adversive stimulus. Therefore, many times, the response results in escape or avoidance behavior. Negative reinforcement is not punishment — many people confuse these two terms. Both negative and positive reinforcement result in an increase in the probability that the behavior that they follow will be strengthened.

Punishment following behavior tends to decrease its future strength (the probability that it will occur). Any event which decreases the strength of behavior that it follows is called a punisher. The only way to determine whether a consequence is a punisher is to observe its effect on the behavior it follows. Punishment is the most effective way to decrease the strength of behavior that is undesired, but it is uneffective in the long run for, although punishment may discontinue the act it wishes to eliminate, as soon as it is removed it is very likely that the undesirable behavior will return. If behaviors are to be reinforced and strengthened, they must be paired with reinforcement. A pupil may avoid punishment by not engaging in behavior that will be punished but he can also avoid punishment by not showing up at school. This is an important reason why teachers and parents should use positive reinforcement rather than punishment. There are cases where punishment is more efficient for the appropriate situation. For example, a parent must punish a child for dashing out into auto traffic, because there is no time for a reinforcement procedure; to do otherwise could result in injury or death of the child. Many patients in institutions mutilate

themselves, and without punishment there is no way to discontinue or control the behavior, or to stop the behavior.

Respondent behavior, or reflex behavior, was brought to
the attention of science by the experiments of Ivan Pavlov.
This kind of behavior is not emitted by the organism, it is
elicited by a stimulus. The reflex of the pupil of the eye,
when light intensity causes it to contract, is a good example
of reflex behavior. The knee jerk reflex is another. Pavlov
showed that the organism could be conditioned to respond
to a neutral stimulus which normally does not elicit a
response when it is coupled with another stimulus which
does elicit a reflex response. He discovered that food elicited
salivation in dogs, and that if a bell was sounded just before
the presentation of food, the sounding of the bell alone
would soon elicit salivation. The food was called an uncond-
tioned stimulus and the salivation a conditioned response.
The bell sound was called a conditioned stimulus and the
salivation following it was a conditioned response. In
summary, respondent conditioning can be achieved by
pairing a neutral stimulus with a conditioned stimulus
until the neutral stimulus also elicits a response. Then the
neutral stimulus is labeled a conditioned stimulus.

Emotional behavior is reflex, or respondent, behavior.
Sometimes children become physically ill when entering or
attending school. To overcome this, it is sometimes
necessary to be sure that punishment or criticism is not
paired with the school environment. This is based on the
fact that if the bell in Pavlov's experiment was repeatedly
rung without pairing it with food, the sound of the bell
would soon loose its eliciting power. This is called
respondent, or reflexive, extinction.

To repeat, random behavior, or voluntary behavior
emitted by an organism, is always controlled by the consequences that follow it. That is the basic principle on which
operant conditioning depends. Behavior followed by a
reinforcing consequence will increase in strength and the

probability that it would re-occur. The only way to verify whether a consequence is reinforcing is to observe the behavior of the organism.

Reinforcement must immediately follow, or overlap, the desired behavior. The quicker, the more effective. In shaping, closer approximations to the target behavior are reinforced. A child who is disorderly at home can be reinforced for being orderly for a half hour, then an hour, followed by an entire period of a day. Punishment is often corrective for decreasing the frequency of undesirable behavior, but the organism may engage in other behavior which is no more appropriate. Punishment sometimes works, but many times does not result in improved behavior.

Continuous reinforcement is a term applied to the kind of reinforcement that follows every desired behavior; it is very effective in the acquisition of new behavior. Intermittent reinforcement is effective in maintaining behavior once it has been established. Satiation is produced by a high reinforcement rate; a pigeon can eat only so much grain. Primary reinforcement reinforces biological needs such as hunger or thirst, conditional reinforcement is paired with primary reinforcement.

The description of how the new behavioral science works sounds disarmingly simple and naive, and because of its simplicity, is not too attractive to those who are seeking intellectuality and "deep" communication. The techniques are powerful, and they put a great burden of responsibility on those who are in a position to use them. Retarded children and institutional youth, some of whom have been labeled hopeless, have been able to learn and improve when the contingencies have been carefully arranged. There is much success with these groups. And there is much promise for the future.

Baby Beethoven in the Jungle

Let us recreate a picture that is familiar to us. We have heard it before, and we are aware of what it evokes, but repeating it sometimes drives home the point of the power of environment. Imagine again Ludwig Von Beethoven dropped in the African jungle at the age of three months. He is found by some primitive tribe and raised by a heavily-breasted African woman living in a thatched hut somewhere deep in the jungle. These people are predators and live by the fruits of the hunt. Their diet includes much vegetation — leaves, herbs, and the variety of green growth that is abundant everywhere. Their rituals would be strange to western eyes; circumcision, the marriage dance, and their manner of mourning at the death of a member of the tribe. Consider:

Little Ludwig is now five years old. There is no way that we can distinguish him, other than by his color, from the rest of his acquaintances; his behavior is that of an authentic African tribesman. At the age of thirteen, he is introduced into the ritual of becoming a man, and years later we see him carrying a spear, deeply involved in the tribal dance.

What is the point of this? As we noted earlier, Beethoven wouldn't have been Beethoven if he wasn't raised in a "Beethoven producing" environment. The environment not only shapes our behavior, but our stature, the way we stand, our attitudes, the way we walk, the way we appear, the lines in our face, and the set of our jaw muscles. If a young, blond freckle-faced American youth of 20 or 21 was deposited, when he was a baby, into the arms of an impoverished Italian peasant family in Southern Italy, he would not only behave differently at the age of 20 or 21, but he would look different; he might be fatter from the pasta diet, he would walk differently, perhaps stoop from carrying heavy loads and doing heavy farm work, and the hand and body gestures that accompanied his language would be "typically Italian".

We are the products of what we have been through and have no control over that. It is a matter of chance or luck, but not really, because "chance" and "luck" are part of a lawful design. What appears to be chance is in reality a part of the plan that we do not understand. If we do not understand a particular pattern or process we are inclined to call it random. But mutations are not random. All occurrences in the universe are lawful; they happen because they are supposed to happen.

To repeat, we are the products of what we have been through. Our genetic inheritance is the product of what the species has been through. All of our genetic-based behavior is the result of years of selection by the environment. This, our physiology, is what has survived. It is not always perfect; there are many life forms on the surface of this planet which are barely surviving, literally dragging their way through life. There are rats, indigenous to one of the Scandinavian countries, whose teeth grow out, and continue to grow right back into their skulls, eventually killing them. Man has many disabilities; he is not the optimum and most efficient machine. What we see is the result of years of selection by the environment. What didn't work was rejected, what worked was accepted. Think of the billions upon billions of organisms that have been exposed to the environment in the past; the ones that didn't survive are not here for us to discuss. All we can see are those that have, and it all seems so perfect, almost as if we were designed for the activities that we choose to perform. We repeat: we do not have arms to do things with, we happen to do those things because we have arms; the giraffe does not have a long neck because the fruit grows high, he eats high-growing fruit *because* he has a long neck.

Since this evolutionary process appears to be helter-skelter, think of what it means. What appears to be helter-skelter is *design*, the way the universe works, the manner in which man works in the technical lab, the way all inventions develop, out of trial and error. Testing is a series of accidents — what works is retained, what doesn't work is rejected. It must be repeated that there is no such thing as creativity. All is discovery, adding up to a series of accidents which appear as if the inventor was "knowledgeable". It is as if the environment is intelligent, since it exercises its role of editorship in rejecting and selecting what it can support and what it cannot.

The concept of cause and effect is outmoded because it implies action before the occurrence. Happenings in nature are not caused, they are simultaneously dependent on other happenings, which is quite different. The correct way to state it would be: *a change in an independent variable is accompanied by a change in a dependent variable.* In the case of reinforced behavior, it expresses itself as a control that the environment instantly exerts over organisms to shape their behavior. It is not a question of an organism emitting a behavior which is followed by a response from the environment; *there is always overlap.*

When an organism emits a behavior that is reinforced, the reinforcement occurs *as* the behavior is being emitted. Otherwise we would have the phenomenon of action at a distance, which means that there was no connection between the two occurrences, an unlawful state of affairs.

Nature abhors a vacuum, we know that. There is no "force" between the north and south poles of a magnet. What we identify as *force* has to be made up of tangible material. It could not be *nothing;* it must be particles. There must be "stuff" there. If it were nothing it could not affect anything. If it were nothing we would have nothing to talk about. Gravity is made up of a rain of matter — it would have to be, otherwise it would have no effect. Light must be something, it cannot be just "waves". We must learn to think of energy as mass and of course the inverse is also true;

mass, stuff, material exists because of its activity and processes. All of which leads to a healthier view of reality.

The *nothing* idea carried further leads us into interesting areas of speculation. If there is no such thing as nothing and the universe is infinitely dense, then there must be "a lot" of matter in the universe. The reason we are not aware of it is because it exists in another time sense, similar to a bullet flashing by. The faster a body moves the less we are aware of it and the less effect it has on us. At critically high speeds it apparently has no effect, like the x-ray radiation passing through us, and the cosmic radiation permeating everything on the surface of our planet. Yes, there *can* be two material things occupying the same space at the same time, because we know that cosmic radiation must be made up of particles, and since the particles are moving through our body, there must be some damage taking place at a lower molecular level.

It is highly probable, and certainly within the realm of possibility, that if we aimed a motion picture camera out into what appears to be empty space, say halfway between our planet and the Moon, with a frame rate of billions of frames per second, our projector would indicate globs of matter floating by. If that is true, then the universe is not only what we see through our telescopes, but it is here all around us.

So what has this to do with Beethoven in the jungle? Actually nothing, but yet everything, because all the concepts discussed in this book are part of one single subject for which we have not yet invented a name. Take a close look at your husband or wife or mother or dear friend and imagine what that person would be like if he or she were born and raised in a primitive Tibetan community in the middle of China. Or if you are Chinese, imagine the opposite; your mother, friend, father, husband or wife born and raised in a small town in the heart of the state of Georgia in the United States. The Beethoven story tells us that what we are is what we've been through, which leads us to the next point: nobody is to be blamed or faulted for his behavior, because if we step back and look at antecedent causes (if we may use that term), we would see the mechanism of conditioning working and understand why individuals can't be blamed.

The New Psychology

Just as we can't blame or assign fault to individuals because we now understand that they are products of a process, we cannot assign credit. People appear to be brave and honorable and have character and integrity and are honest and trustworthy and moral and good, but they are simply acting out their shaped behavior as it was shaped by a "chancey" environment in their past. Now that we know this, why leave it to chance? There is no good reason why behavioral science should not try to design optimum environments for developing happier humans. It is inevitable. Questions like, "Who will control?" and "How do we know it will be to our benefit?" and "What is to protect us against totalitarianism?" are based on our value systems of today. We cannot judge the values of tomorrow by ourselves and our own apprehensions. People change, and when the environment is ready, it will create the conditions necessary for the change. What doesn't work will not support a dictator, and what is unpleasant will lead to revolution. How do we know that the pilot in command of a modern passenger aircraft is not evil and leading us to our death? He wants to live also.

Utopias have been attempted before by idealists who had no knowledge of the principles of behavioral science. We are learning a lot today. True, we are studying other species — pigeons and mice. Is the information that we are getting from these experiments transferable to man? Certainly, because we are all structurally related, more closely related than one imagines. Medical research utilizes these animals to test new drugs before they are tried on man, so there must be some similarity in our makeup. Let us not dismiss those experiments too quickly because of their simplicity; for some reason complexity always appears more attractive to man. A lot of jargon published in the field of humanistic psychology utilizes terms like *awareness*, *peak experience*, *getting in touch with reality*, and *meaningful relationship*. None of it is effective if the environment does not change. Man is under the control of his environment, and to treat him in an office for an hour and return him to that environment accomplishes little.

Many of us are being kept from climbing the walls through tranquilization and drugs. We've all heard of the *thorazine shuffle*, patients blissfully shuffling up and down hospital wards, well-tranquilized and sweetly docile. But that delays the answer by temporarily putting a hold on the problem. Curiously, sometimes the techniques of psychotherapy do have value, but when they work they work for other than the reasons described. They work because they happen to be applying behavioral principles. For instance, insight into our difficulties turns us into another person because when we monitor or log our behavior from hour to hour, day after day, we become observers and investigators. We have become other people, and as a result we change and improve. This technique is used to break smoking habits. It is also the mechanism which explains how insight into our problems works, and psychotherapy sometimes comes off luckily, although the technique gropes. It gropes because its premise is fallacious; there are no stored experiences of our childhood inside of us. There are no past conflicts buried there to disturb us. We are simply changed individuals, changed by experience, and the only way to change us again is by new experience.

People do not act because they feel angry or hungry, they act and feel for other reasons. When we think we are free, the environmental controls are not obvious, but subtle. There is no such phenomenon as freedom; everything in nature is under control at all times. It is ironic, but when the cause of a person's behavior is obvious, we do not blame him. For instance, if he is born crippled we condone the deviance because the reason is obvious. When less conspicuous forms of heredity cause trouble we assign fault. If we do not punish a person for obvious genetic difficulties, why do we punish him for being aggressive, where this might have been caused by some subtle genetic factor? Punishment cannot change our genetic inheritance; we can only make changes through genetic control in the laboratory. The same idea applies to what happens in the environment. When we hear that poor people are genetically inclined toward poverty, we know that the lack of advantage is the cause.

We must think of our familiar terms another way. What we call *psychological depression* today is something else; it is an example of a very low reinforcement rate. *Anxiety* is emotional behavior induced by a history of aversive behavioral consequences. *Guilt* is an emotional response to a history of punishment or failure. *Neuroticism* is a range of ineffective behaviors attempting to escape an aversive situation. We cannot simply *motivate* people, we have to design environments in which they will acquire behavior useful to them and our society. *Corruption in government* is not to be blamed on the "Watergaters", it is the set of conditions which give rise to Watergates which should be changed. What should be manipulated is the world in which nations make war; it is a waste of time to talk about *international tension.*

Chained to the Money System

Why is it that we are not seeing a public and scientific awareness to the new approaches? Why is there not a dramatic move in this direction? The money system under which we live is responsible for the prevailing attitude. It is not possible to control environments today, to build large, planned, efficiently laid out, circular cities with beautiful suburbs, green and clean. Who would finance it? Who would profit? Who would be the select citizenry to live there, and how could it survive as an island in the middle of our archaic money system?

The engineering of society will come when the money system fails, as it surely must. It is failing already; we are too close to see it. The system is only working for the affluent and even for the affluent it provides a large measure of insecurity. They are breathing the same air and are subject to the same threat of nuclear destruction. We are all the same people. If we walk down the street of a typical American suburb in late evening and look into the windows of most homes, we see entire families staring passively at the tube; families are staring vacantly at the same tubes in the affluent sections as in the poor sections of the city. Each of us is subject to the same televised conditioning processes today. Our value systems are much the same; largely molded by television, radio, and newspapers. The definition of what is news is imposed upon us. Most of what is in the newspapers has no significance to our lives; it is entertainment, show business, titillation, escape, and public relations — an advanced form of back fence gossip. Socially significant events on a world scale are rarely reported without sensationalism or bias, and invariably from the point of view of our money system. International terrorism and the media were made for each other; the news people need the panic and the terrorists need the publicity.

In April, 1964, David Brinkley, TV news commentator, said to *TV Guide:* "News is what *I* say it is. It's something worth knowing by *my* standards." TV news programs are the result of an incredible chain of such selective processes; the jargon, the subtle implications in the scripts and the inferences of announcers, the money system bias, the political stress, the personal opinions of news writers, all cut and fit to provide an entertaining 22-minute show. And its effect is more than entertainment; it helps shape and mold the opinions, attitudes, values, and lifestyles of the many millions of helpless people who are subjected daily to the powerful control of these merchants of panic.

What we won't hear on television or read in the newspapers is that our technology will dispense with business, finance, and politics. The area most blessed for the first social application of science will most likely be the United States and its neighboring countries because of its energy resources. The abundance that that technology is producing is alone disintegrating the money system because without scarcity there can be no politics, no business, and no finance.

Yes, the welfare state has slowed the demise of the money system, and it will continue to help the system endure. To keep the poor and the disenfranchised on short rations is playing a kind of brinkmanship, but so far it has paid off; there is restlessness and gripe, but not revolution. In spite of the reason that it exists, there is no question that unemployment insurance, social security, Medicare, welfare, old age pensions, and the like, notwithstanding some flaws, have made life bearable for millions.

And what a gravy train it has been for others: corruption at the federal and local levels and out-and-out stealing by doctors, pharmacists, and nursing homes have bled the till white — far more than the occasional cheating by reported Cadillac-driving welfare recipients.

Welfare in the United States is a mere pittance of the support accorded the poor in some European countries. When we think of the American public's support of the deception and waste of our advertising and Pentagon budgets, and their converse attitude toward health care budgets, we can begin to realize the extent to which the public has been conditioned to act against its own interest. That predicament furnishes us with a remarkable example of the powers of mass conditioning.

The behaviorists are right.

From Witchcraft
to Spacecraft

7

When the proofs, the figures, were ranged in
  columns before me;
When I was shown the charts and the diagrams, to
  add, divide, and measure them
When I, sitting, heard the astronomer, where he
  lectured with much applause in the lecture-room,
How, soon, unaccountable, I became tired and sick;
Till rising and gliding out, I wander'd off
  by myself,
In the mystical moist night-air, and
  and from time to time,
Look'd up in perfect silence at the stars.

Walt Whitman

To look at the clear computer-generated photos taken by the Viking-Mars Lander on the surface of Mars is a mystic experience, and it takes a slight jump of imagination to place ourselves on the planet. The photos are high-resolution closeups of various areas around the landing site. We can even see the rivets and the Martian dust on the Lander foot pad. There is a photograph of a ditch which is about 31 feet long and 6 inches deep, made up of fine sediment; it is possible that this particular soil structure is the result of the cyclic freezing and thawing of ground water. If trenches such as these on the surface of Mars are indicative of the sub-surface formation of ice as they would be on the planet Earth, then their formation must have occurred a long time ago when the liquid water was stable. With the

113

present atmosphere, liquid water would either freeze or boil away. Among the pictures are large wide-angle Martian panoramas, all rock-strewn and barren of life. There are mounds which appear to be sand dunes but are probably made up of finer grain, of silt and clay. It does not appear that these dunes are of the type that one associates with deserts. Instead, they appear to be the stabilized remnants of the erosion of a more extensive sediment coverage.

The thrill that we feel as we look at these pictures and imagine ourselves landing on Mars is generated by our loneliness in this world. In the black void nine planets spin silently around that ball of flame we call the Sun. And light years away are billions upon billions of other suns similar in many respects to ours; some of them older, some younger. It is like a giant bowling alley of meaningless absurdity. What? Why? What is this riddle that we contemplate? There is no doubt that we will one day walk on the surface of Mars and travel through the solar system, to orbit other planets and land on them. Or instead of travelling in person, we may choose to travel remotely, with camera and instrumentation more sensitive than the sensory system of man himself.

What we think of as magic we know is illusion, yet magic is possible. Science has given us magic. We are surrounded by it in our everyday world of artifacts. We take these artifacts for granted, true, but they are magic nonetheless. A small hand-held transistor radio is magic in the sense that out of it can come the sounds of a symphony concert which at that very moment is playing thousands of miles away. That is magic. Magic is not possible in certain frames of reference, while it is possible in other frames of reference. For instance, we know that a ventriloquist's claim of being able to "throw" his voice across a room so that it appears to come out of the mouth of somebody else is not true and not possible, as stated. Yet, through technology, one can "throw" his voice via radio transmission and make it appear anywhere he wishes, with the use of remote microphones and hand-held transmitters.

It would be magic if we could fly but we, as humans, cannot fly. The magic came in the forms of airplanes, helicopters, and soon levicraft, which will be based on the principle of a kind of magic levitation, or antigravity machine.

What is going on today in the world of microprocessors and computers is magic. Machines that think — yes, artificial intelligence is coming. Will it stop? It cannot, because technological development always moves forward. There is no end to design, and there is no end to improvement. There is no final *best* way to do something, because someone will soon come along to top it. So the world of magic that the astrologers and the ESP and flying saucer addicts are looking for is either here or will be here through the scientific method, because anything is possible in science.

But some things are not possible because we try to make them come true in the wrong ways. We can't shout into a tube and capture our voice, hoping to release it later. Yet, we can make a recording of our voice, which is the same kind of magic. To communicate with intelligent civilizations on alien planets is not possible. The existence of intelligent species on alien planets is also not possible. It cannot be, for the reasons given above, and yet through science anything is possible.

Scientific investigation of the nature of "communication" and the nature of "intelligence" will force the terms *communication* and *intelligence* out of our language and advance us to a new understanding of the processes of the universe. A milestone will have been achieved as soon as we realize that what appears to be intelligence and awareness in our own humans on this planet are not, that they are not magically motivating themselves about, but are controlled and moved by unseen and subtle forces.

Yes, we know there is no magic, that there must be an explanation for everything. When we understand a phenomenon, it ceases to be magical and we can then control it, and when we can control it we can manipulate it, and when we can manipulate it we can say that we understand it.

Planet Earth, with all of us as passengers, and the rest of our solar system, with its family of planets, satellites, meteors, comets, tiny particles, and giant globs of matter, are rushing along through the cosmos at a speed of over a million miles a day to some point in space, we know not where. And we don't appear to be getting any closer, for we have been hanging on to the coat-tails of our Sun on this wild ride for millions of years. That is magic, because we cannot yet control it.

From another coordinate system, another point of view, our entire solar system is just a tiny particle moving through space. But from the point of view of we people on Earth, our sun is the big mother on whom we depend for continual sustenance.

Of billions upon billions upon billions upon billions (we could go on infinitely) of stars, our sun appears to be the only one which possesses planets, although we feel it unlikely that it could be unique in that respect. Orbiting around our sun, in addition to our planets, are chunks of iron and stone which are known as meteors. When one of these enters our atmosphere, their high speed generates friction which causes them to glow brightly. Sometimes we call these falling stars.

Comets regularly orbit the sun, mostly in elliptical patterns, and a large part, but not all, of the light that we see glowing from their luminous tails is reflected sunlight. Comets are made up of a coma which may be 150,000 miles in diameter, a nucleus, and sometimes a tail, a magical stream of gaseous matter seldom less than 5 million magical miles long.

The distance between our solar system and the other stars is measured in light years, the distance light travels in one year, about 6 trillion miles. The *parsec* is used as a unit of distance where even the light year would be too small a unit to use. A parsec equals 3.258 light years. A *mega-parsec* is equal to 1,000,000 parsecs, or 3,258,000 light years. Try to imagine the speed of light: a trip to the Moon at the speed of light would take 1¼ seconds, to the Sun 8 minutes, to Neptune 4 hours, to our nearest star 4½ years. To ?, ????

Our sun is a member of a galaxy of other suns in a mystic family known as the Milky Way, which is shaped like a disc with spiral arms, and whose size is about 30,000 pc (parsecs), or 100,000 light years, in diameter. Our sun is located about half way from the center of this disc and, in an act of pure witchery, moves at a speed of approximately 200 miles per second about the disc center, taking about 200 million years to complete one revolution — all of this while the galaxy rotates.

Astronomers have assigned a series of numbers to the suns (stars), which define their brightness, or brilliance. Star brilliance is determined by two factors, their distance from us and their true brilliance. Stars are classified as 1st magnitude, 2nd magnitude, etc., up to 20th magnitude, the higher numbers designating less brilliancy. Betelgeuse in the constellation Orion, Deneb in Cygnos, and Aldebaran in Taurus are examples of 1st magnitude stars.

Stars also vary in color and size. Spectroscopy tells us that their color is linked to their age, their place in evolutionary time, and their size and surface brilliancy. Sizes of stars range from sorcerers millions of miles in diameter to enchanting dwarfs, a few thousands of miles in diameter.

There are other variations such as multiple stars which are groups of two or more stars, variable stars which vary in magnitude periodically, and Novas which are new stars that appear relatively suddenly and fade slowly.

Aside from our Milky Way there are galaxies too

numerous to number, each containing billions of stars, each star a sun like our own. There are approximately a billion galaxies within reach of the 200-inch telescope on Mt. Palomar, most of them grouped into clusters.

Galaxies and galactic clusters abound in every direction. Our galaxy, the Milky Way, belongs to an exclusive cluster society, the Local Group, which contains about 17 member galaxies and measures about 3 million light years in diameter. The two largest members of the Local Group are both spiral galaxies — our own Milky Way, and M31, Andromeda.

The universe is continually expanding, a fact we have determined from the radial velocities of the galaxies. This suggests that, in a feat of polished legerdemain, an "explosion" occurred, starting the galaxies moving away from each other. As the universe is expanding, it is thinning out, and if all the mass in the universe is constant — that is, if new matter is not being created continuously — then all of the matter once must have been together. This cosmological model is called the "Big Bang" theory. The age of the universe, according to this theory, is calculated from the speed of recession of the galaxies, as they explode away from the source. That age is estimated to lie in the range of 12 to 18 billion years.

The other cosmological model of the universe, known as the "Steady State" theory, states that the universe was always here, and is the same everywhere, at all times. The theory explains that, as the universe expands and the galaxies separate, new matter is continually created, which maintains the mean density at a constant level.

Both models of the universe are based on assumptions that will most likely turn out to be just as primitive as the notions of the early Greek philosophers. In the meantime, our space sciences move forward, and soon we shall see radical changes in our theories, as our instrumentation and delivery techniques become ever more refined.

Searching the universe by microwave extends our view by a large factor. Sources of microwave radiation in the universe are few compared to the billions of sources of light energy. But the most distant sources of light energy that we can detect with our telescopes are a paltry two billion light years away. On the other hand, radio telescopes are presently detecting microwave radiation from sources that far outstrip the range of optical telescopes. Among these sources are 3C48, 3C147, 3C196, 3C273, and 3C286 — 3C standing for the *3rd Cambridge Catalog of Radio Stars*. 3C273, among others, has been analyzed spectroscopically and found to be receding at a velocity of 25,000 miles per second. Other sources have been discovered to be receding at comparable expansion rates, presumably caused by the big fat bang. These sources are now referred to as *radio galaxies* rather than radio stars.

Because of recent advances in rocket and satellite technology and the contribution of radio telescopes, we are becoming increasingly aware of new magic in the universe. "Quasi-stellar" phenomena (which we contract to form the word *quasar)* and black holes are discussed daily in our press.

The existence of *black holes* is theoretical, but the evidence suggests that their existence is highly probable. A massive collapsing star becomes so increasingly dense that its gravity eventually does not permit any matter, including light, to leave. Light particles, or photons, which magically escape, are forced to arc in a curved path and return. As a result, the star remains dark to our telescopes, but its X-ray radiation and microwave emissions have been detected by satellite-borne instrumentation. There is little known, but there is much speculation, about black holes; but we do know that they exist, that there are many of them, and that they are the result of the collapse of a super-giant neutron star.

What is the basic stuff of which the universe is made? For

that, we must look in the other direction, toward the atom, a direction that is as limitless as the universe out there. Here we have true magic. Particles smaller than the atom are the target of everyday research in scientific laboratories. We hear talk of pixie-like *neutrinos*, of *charm*, and of *quark*, which are all very real in the way they affect our instrumentation. Our galaxy consists of about 130,000,000,000 stars, among which is our own sun, which compares to the rest as a speck of dust. And beyond our galaxy there are billions of other galaxies reaching out toward infinity, just as the universe reaches down toward infinity in the other direction, the direction of the atom.

The relationship of these sub-atomic particles to the universe is so important that the study of them has given birth to a new sorcery called neutrino astronomy, or particle astronomy. The mystic world of antiparticles, of liptons and baryons, of alpha particle analysis, of neutrinos and antineutrinos, of the particle building blocks of the universe, is revealing itself to research physicists to be as vast an area of study as astronomy. And just as it is necessary to understand all disciplines to avoid traps in our thinking, we are discovering that to understand the basic processes of the magical birth and death of stars it is necessary to understand sub-particle physics.

An Extraterrestrial
8   Critique

The mystique of phILOSophy, bathed in an irreproachable celestial light, is obsolete. Many of our undeniably brilliant phILOSophers remain hopelessly trapped in their narrow specialties as they view the world through kaleidoscopically-colored glasses. It is high time that TRAP 1 thinking, like the elephant of fable, dragged itself off to some distant jungle graveyard and died. Our phILOSophers have outlived their usefulness; their concepts are distorted, and their high-sounding comments are perfect examples of the doctrine of immanence. Here is an overview of the state-of-the-art of phILOSophy today, whose ranks embrace not only scientists, but businessmen, lawyers, anthropologists, and many others.

Voodoo Yes — Surgery No

If you had an acute attack of appendicitis and had to be rushed to a hospital for emergency surgery, would you rather go on the back of a donkey or by high-speed ambulance? To choose the donkey would not be intelligent by anybody's definition. Yet, here are the words of Freeman Dyson, quoted in *The Galactic Club:* "I make a sharp distinction between intelligence and technology. *It is easy to imagine* a highly intelligent society with no particular interest in technology." (Emphasis added.)

It is difficult to imagine an intelligent society which would prefer to trudge a mile to a well with bucket-in-hand than turn on a faucet, or choose a hand-held torch over a flashlight, or opt for a smoke signal rather than a telephone, or pick voodoo over modern medicine, and so forth. Pure TRAP 5. Unless, by *intelligence*, Dyson is referring to a kind of philosophically-profound "enlightenment". Philosophy leads to the nescience which we acquire after years of sitting in a rocking chair speculating about the universe. Technology equals intelligence and intelligence equals technology.

Blythe Spirits

R. Buckminster Fuller, who is known as the Leonardo Da Vinci of our time, provides us with an illustration of his genius. In the following quotes, taken from *Worlds Beyond*, Mr. Fuller tells us that:

1. "No machines will ever be intelligent. They never have been and never will be."

2. "There is a physical universe and a metaphysical universe . . . . . your whole intellect is utterly metaphysical . . . . . that's why cybernetic intelligence is a contradiction in terms."

3. "What is really going on is that the *mind is discovering the principles of brain to be only a special case* . . . . ." (Emphasis his, not ours.)

We could continue, but taken totally, those three statements, all perfect specimens of poetic non-scientific language, could only appeal to the devotees of extraterrestrial fiction. Man is a highly complex machine. He could be nothing else but a machine. As computers evolve, they will not only catch up to us, but surpass us. If we are all machines, then Buckminster Fuller must be a machine. And if Buckminster Fuller is a machine, his first statement may indeed be true of all of us.

A Prophet of Profit

J. Peter Vajk, a well-known research physicist concerned with the social implications of space colonization, talks to us from TRAP 1 in this excerpt from *Doomsday Has Been Cancelled*. As many futurists do, he peers into the future and sees only the trees and not the forest. Everything will change but dollars and cents and profit and loss; the picture he paints is of a new world still burdened by the vestigial remains of the money system, with financiers, businessmen, lawyers, and politicians rampant. Here he is talking about communications satellites: ". . . . . assuming reasonable rates of market penetration . . . . . we expect this company could have annual revenues between ten and twenty billion dollars. Large satellites like this are a sure bet to go." And later, he says, about space satellites: ". . . . . the chances are excellent that there will be large profits to be made."

If what he says becomes a reality, then we should despair for the human race. There will be a place in space for the scientist and even the non-scientist but, fortunately, the March of Events will spare us the politician and businessman. Also, the vague term *profit*, like *price* or *value*, should have no place in a scientific discussion. *Webster's International Dictionary* (2nd edition) weakly defines *profit* as "The share of the employing classes in the distribution of the products of industry as distinct from *wages*, which constitutes the share of the laboring classes — covering interest, insurance for risk, and wages of superintendence. (Others say) that profit . . . . . does not include either interest or insurance, but represents the reward of the employer for his skill, as distinct from that of the capitalist for his saving. This view is now the one generally prevalent." Confusing?

In science all statements are definable and verifiable. There is no argument among scientists on the definition of a centimeter. At the International Bureau of Standards in France there is a platinum bar stored in a room whose temperature is maintained at 0° centigrade. On this bar there are two scratched lines one meter apart. A centimeter is defined as one-hundredth the distance between these lines. If terms or concepts cannot be defined the "centimeter way", we can verify their existence and measure them by their effect on sensitive instrumentation. We use oscilloscopes, telescopes, microscopes, spectral analysis, and many other extensions of our senses to verify phenomena in the real world. The velocity of light has been checked, verified, tested, and measured by many different techniques and instruments, and it never fails to come out 2.997925 plus or minus 0.000002 x 10^{10} centimeters per second or 186,000 miles per second.

At a recent seminar on the industrial uses of space, one of the topics on the agenda dealt with the possibility of attractive tax-free advantages in space-generated profits. It seems that SETI, which is an acronym used by the phILOSophers for the Search for ExtraTerrestrial Intelligence, has taken on a new meaning in some circles: the Search for Extended Tax-free Income. Dr. Vajk, as most futurists, will have us believe that tomorrow's social system will be the same as today's — where the rich continue to inherit money for which they do no work while millions live in poverty. If today's scientists see that science must be applied to our social system as well as our satellites, they could not say, as Gerard O'Neill says, in *Worlds Beyond:* "If you ask me what I suspect is going to be the government of space habitats, I suspect we'll find every form of government we've had on the surface of the Earth, *including the bad ones.*" (Emphasis ours.)

A Capital Idea

G. Harry Stine, author, consulting engineer, marketing man, model rocketeer, and pilot, says in the book, *Worlds Beyond:* "To be absolutely crude about it, we've got to figure out how to make a buck in space so that we can have space." And then, "I'm a consultant in high-technology marketing. I'm applying marketing techniques to space industrialization." Why not first apply a few of those marketing techniques to the fiscal state of our nation? We recommend that Mr. Stine postpone his dream until after our budget is balanced and all income and social security taxes have been reduced to zero.

Res Judicata

Where entrepreneurs, financiers, and politicians go, the lawyers cannot be far behind, as announced to us by Ina Risman in *Worlds Beyond:* "As people venture into space ... they will need to have all facets of their existence be equitably managed. (This will) cover everything from assignment of liability for damages to persons or equipment, to property settlement between two space inhabitants bound in marriage." At least that. In space we will need lawyers for wills, bankruptcy, personal injury, leases, divorce, annulment, contracts, real estate, taxes, profits, adoptions, libel, slander, medical malpractice, and legal malpractice. And more — separate maintenance, how to minimize taxes, how to avoid probate, and more.

AnthropOMORPHology

Anthropologists have also joined the space chorus. They intend to be there, to act as consultants, when our culture meets the alien culture, so that neither group will offend the other by some unintended rudeness or insult. Some of them, with "space" lawyers to help them, are already working on drafting provisions in "metalaw", which will guarantee physical security for us and them, a sort of SALT treaty in the sky. Anthropologist Barbra Moskowitz warns us that we must observe them before we make physical contact; if they consider us a threat they will probably be represented by one of their military leaders; if they believe we are representatives of a God we will most likely be asked to meet with their clergy. Anthropomorphic anthropology should be labeled *anthropomorphology.*

It Seems Reasonable to Assume

The five points following, charged with an antiquated animism*, were taken from the *Stanford/NASA/Ames Project Cyclops Report.* Our indented comment follows each point:

". . . . . it seems reasonable to assume that:

1. Most civilizations at some point in their development perçeive the likelihood of other life in the universe, as we do, and find themselves technically able to search for and signal that life, as we are."

> Civilizations, at some *later* point, begin to ask questions about the meaning of perception. They then

---

*(an' i mizm) The belief that objects possess a life or vitality or are endowed with indwelling souls. Such life is not only ascribed to men, but to animals, plants, trees, stones, and others.

discover that the entire corpus of their science exists only because of its effect on them, that *perception is behavior*, and its existence can only be demonstrated by the behavior from which it is inferred. At that point, they discard animism and move to higher ground.

"2. Many civilizations decide on an active search strategy."

Pogo said: "We have met the enemy and he is us." Technically-advanced civilizations who may be unwise enough to search the universe for "intelligent life" will say, at the end of their long journey: "We have searched for aliens and have found ourselves."

"3. Many of the earliest to do so followed their search phase with a radiative phase and were subsequently detected."

No matter how they explain it, the word *detected*, as the phILOSophers use it here, can only mean detection by other humans, other civilizations playing the same hide-and-seek games we are. See TRAPS 1, 2, 4, and 5 in Chapter 1.

"4. Success in one contact led to:
a. Great intellectual excitement and social benefits.
b. A sustained effort at further contacts."

That statement falls into the same category as the anthropomorphic plaque riding aboard Pioneer 10, with the man's right arm raised in "friendly" greeting. Try raising your right arm in friendly greeting in front of a cage full of hungry monkeys. What if our space alien siblings don't have a sense of humor?

"5. As a late entry, we are heirs to the fruits of all successful past efforts, including beacons to attract attention."

The model sketched for us here is of a universe made up of two disconnected properties. Property 1: The stars and the planets and the comets and the meteor showers and gravitation and the space-time continuum and the big hot bang and light energy and radiation and much more. Property 2: The civilizations who observe, study, research, explore, communicate, phILOSophize, and finally solve, the riddle of Property 1. The sophisticated scientists of these civilizations then get together at a giant universal seminar in the sky and share the secrets of Property 1 — how Property 1 began, how Property 1 will end, and so on. And this is not whimsy. We found it, all written down, in a serious proposal for research money submitted to a government of politicians who are even more confused by the entire subject than the scientists are.

Planet Earth is four and one-half billion years old. Many solar systems are at least 10 to 15 billion years old. Any messages we receive from them could have been sent before Columbus discovered America, before the putative birth of Christ, even before planet Earth was born. Those civilizations are long dead and gone, even if they once existed, which is not possible.

A Brief Log of Contact Activities

The idea of listening for microwave transmissions from alien civilizations was first suggested by Philip Morrison and Guiseppe Cocconi in 1959. Frank Drake's *Project Ozma*, in 1960, was the first organized try at it. Aiming at Tau Ceti and Epsilon Eridani, he listened for 150 hours before the experiment was abandoned.

Gerrit Verschuur tried again in 1972, extending Drake's work to ten nearby stars, but to no avail. The most ambitious search to date was made in 1976 by Ben Zuckerman and Patrick Palmer, who surveyed 659 stars.

Frank Drake and Carl Sagan have been using the 305 meter antenna at Arecibo, Puerto Rico to listen for messages. They have been scanning nearby galaxies, but so far have not detected any telltale signs. Robert Dixon and Dennis Cole of the Ohio State University Radio Observatory have been sweeping the sky with a receiver more sensitive than most. Dixon is also associated with *Cosmic Search*, a magazine devoted to the search for intelligent life in space.

There is a 26 meter antenna at the Hat Creek observatory staffed by astronomers from the University of California at Berkeley. Also, NASA and the Jet Propulsion Laboratory in California are jointly engaged in the design of a Multi-Channel Spectral Analyzer. The MCSA will have one million channels, utilizing microprocessor technology which enables them to considerably reduce the size of the pathway. They are now thinking in terms of a billion channel MCSA.

There are searches going on in other countries as well, including the Soviet Union. And the pace of the search is increasing. In November, 1974, the first message with content and meaning was beamed from the 305 meter dish at Arecibo, simultaneously covering about 300,000 stars. It was the most powerful signal radiated up that point, consisting of a string of 1679 pulses which the receiving civilization would have to rearrange into a roster of 23 x 73 characters, forming a graphic image containing much information: our counting system, a schematic of the DNA double helix, pictures of a human, the Arecibo dish, five atoms (hydrogen, oxygen, nitrogen, carbon, and phosphorus), and other useful information for space aliens.

In August and September of 1977, Voyagers 1 and 2 were launched, to drift forever among the stars with the same kind of useful information aboard as the Pioneer probes with their anthropomorphic drawings. Each probe carried a 12-inch diameter long-playing record designed to be played at a speed of 16-2/3 rpm. A cartridge, needle, and instructions were provided for the convenience of the space aliens. The records contain 115 pictures electronically encoded into the grooves, a message from President Carter, greetings from around the earth in 55 languages, the story of evolution with sound effects (the dawn of man is accompanied by footsteps and heartbeats), and the sounds of technology, from space vehicle launchings to the beat of a pulsar. An extra attraction is 90 minutes of music, from pan pipes and Indian chants to Bach, Beethoven, Louis Armstrong, and Chuck Berry.

There is considerably more search activity going on than we have covered in this sketchy outline. Any aliens out there with patience enough to wait years for an answer to their putative message deserve the attempts being made on Earth to make contact with them.

In addition to the programmed searches, there is a powerful earth-bound microwave beacon sweeping the universe: the leakage from our military radar and our television transmitters. Anybody out there who is determined to hear us has a good chance of intercepting one of our TV programs. Fortunately for them, it is unlikely our programs would make any more sense to them than they do to us.

The Second Coming

The UFOnauts depicted in the reported contacts made by we earth people must be awfully dumb, or not as advanced as we think they are. They have made many bad landings, and their attempts to communicate with us have been rather sketchy and not too clear. But to the UFOlogists, their comings and goings are like the nativity, the resurrection, and the Second Coming all rolled into one, so we must never question their existence.

And we had better not question the existence of the agoraphobic aliens who stayed behind, who chose not to venture forth on their saucers. That is a sacred article of faith to the many phILOSophers kneeling at the microwave altar, each one secretly hoping to be the first to make contact. Their technology is outstanding and, aside from the popularizers and sensationalists, their motives are beyond question; they are mostly dedicated scientists quietly working on what is to them an exciting program. But what they are looking for is a person, a fellow scientist, an externalization of their false concept of themselves. What has evolved on this planet is simply an organism, part of the behavior of which is explained by the invention of a mythical mind. We are more mediocre than they would have us imagine, and a great deal less "advanced". No special talent is needed to understand this when the facts are considered on their own merits.

Our Internal Eyes and Ears

Carl Sagan, in *The Dragons of Eden*, says that "Human ritual and emotional behavior are certainly influenced strongly by neocortical abstract reasoning; analytical demonstrations of the validity of purely religious beliefs have been proferred, and there are philosophical justifications for hierarchical behavior, such as Thomas Hobbes' 'demonstration' of the divine right of kings. Likewise, animals that are not human — and in fact even some animals that are not primates — seem to show glimmerings of analytical abilities." He goes on to say: ". . . . . the

altruistic, emotional, and religious aspects of our lives to be
localized to a significant extent in the limbic system and
shared with our nonprimate mammalian forebearers (and
perhaps the birds); and reason to be a function of the
neocortex, shared to some extent with the higher primates
and such cetaceans as dolphins and whales. While ritual,
emotion, and reasoning are all significant aspects of human
nature, the most nearly unique human characteristic is the
ability to associate abstractly and to reason."

That quotation is a classic example of assigning the
behavior of an organism to some spontaneously generating
computerized system, an example of animism and
spiritualism in modern dress. This is the old view: that man
is a shell, and peering out of his eyeballs is a super-sophis-
ticated computer which receives inputs, processes and
synthesizes information, and acts as a way station for the
distribution of functions and processes within and without.
It is not true. Certainly something is happening within our
heads but the cause of our behavior lies without. There is no
decision-making or processing of information taking place;
the behavior of an organism is determined by its genetic
endowment and its conditioning. If we say that reason is a
function of the neocortex then we must say also that the
movement of plants is the result of reason. Otherwise one
must believe that man is special, unique, and somehow
different from the other life forms and species that inhabit
our planet.

Sagan again, from *The Dragons of Eden:* "We can
approach the question of the information content of the
human brain in a quite different way — introspectively.
Try to imagine some visual memory, say from your
childhood. Look at it very closely in *your mind's eye.*
Imagine it is composed of a set of fine dots like a newspaper
wirephoto. Each dot has a certain color and brightness. You
must now ask how many bits of information are necessary to
characterize the color and brightness of each dot; how many

dots make up the recall picture; and how long it takes to recall all the details of the picture in *the eye of the mind*. In this retrospective, you focus on a very small part of the picture at any one time; your field of view is quite limited. When you put in all these numbers, you come out with a rate of information processing by the brain, in bits per second. When I do such a calculation, I come out with a peak processing rate of about 5,000 bits per second." (Emphasis added.) In ancient Greece they believed that humans could not capture and possess the real world but they could certainly make copies of it; it could be memorized and retrieved at will and acted upon anytime they felt like it. In the preceding quotation we have this same outmoded view presented to us by a contemporary scientist in 1977. The information theory and computer analogy does not hold up; the world does not enter the head, is not translated or transduced, is not stored, and does not emerge at the will of the human. The world does not enter through the eye and generate a process that results in vision, later transforming that image into a perception. The world remains where it always was — outside the body.

There is no *tabula rasa* in the head, the brain does not process data or make choices or decisions; it is the whole person who does these things. Persons respond to current stimuli because of their exposure to shaping processes of which that stimuli has been a part. There is no evidence that there is stored information which is retrievable by some inside file clerk. It is interesting that the internal copy idea was discarded more than 2,000 years ago by Theophrastus, as quoted by B.F. Skinner in his book, *About Behaviorism:* ". . . . . with regard to hearing . . . . . he has ascribed the process to internal sounds and assumed that the ear produces a sound within like a bell. By means of this internal bell we might hear sounds without, but how should we hear this internal sound itself? The old problem would still confront us."

For the same reason, we wonder how we can see a picture in the cortex of the brain unless we had an eye inside our head. When a person is hearing a piece of music "in his head" when it is not actually being played, he is simply doing some of the things he did when it was being played; it is a case of low-level behavior. When a person sees something in his imagination, he is not scanning an internal screen with an inner eye, he is simply doing what he does when he sees that something in the real world. In a dream, a person is not an audience-of-one watching a theatrical production; he is involved in the same kinds of behavior he would be in actual life. Dream research supports this contention. The middle ear is activated when dreams involve audition. This is not physiological input into the dream, it *is* the dream.

Skinner in *About Behaviorism*, is quoting Plato: "A man cannot inquire either about that which he knows or about that which he does not know; for if he knows he has no need to inquire; and if not, he cannot, for he does not know the very subject about which he is to inquire." If we are able to remember something there is no need to search our memory file. If we are unable to remember it, how can we find it? We must stop thinking in terms of libraries, warehouses of information, postal systems, transportation systems, and computers inside our little heads. What affects organisms is not stored. What affects organisms changes the organisms. The result is that organisms behave differently after an experience.

Pictures at an Exhibition

The computer model does not work. It is as elementary as the *tabula rasa* idea. It is as ancient as the idea of the homunculus, the inner person who was blamed for the behavior of the outer person in ancient times. Thinking is behavior, and not an inner process which expresses itself in behavior. Isaac Asimov, an inner, as well as an outer space expert, says in a N.Y. Times article *Pills to Help Us Remember:* "I have a clear map of the United States imprinted in my mind and I can look at it and copy off the names of all the states as fast as I can write." What he is doing is behaving as he does when he sees a.real map of the United States; he is not looking at a screen projection inside of his head. It is this approach and these concepts that lead to speculations about extraterrestrial forms of life.

It is easy to see how it happens. Observing a bird in flight, it is difficult to imagine that the bird is not controlling his flight and navigating where he chooses. It is difficult to picture the environment as controlling every movement of the bird. Watching a large bird flare out and flutter into a soft landing on a telephone wire seems to indicate that he knows what he is doing, that he is a wise old bird. But we must acknowledge that the concept of the spontaneous generation of behavior or the spontaneous generation of anything is fallacious and that everything must be moved and controlled by the medium in which it lives. That awareness brings us forward to a new place in our view of the universe — a realization that we are the products of everything around us and that we are moved and controlled by them. When we observe a limb flutter in the breeze there is a tendency to believe that it knows what it is doing. When we watch leaves turn toward the light or observe germs through a microscope they seem to have intention or will, but if we suspend the notion of projecting ourselves into everything we see, we can then see more truthfully, and more usefully.

All is controlled, even in what appears to be a free and uncontrolled environment. The cradle acts as a controller in a child's development. The child's room and all the artifacts which civilizations have used to rear children: rattles, balls, dolls, and the other gadgetry that surround cribs are critical shaping devices that determine later behavior. At a later stage the rocking horse, the walker, and harness systems act as controllers. The question is really one of complexity; human systems, like all other systems in the universe, are actually limitless continuums of changes.

The Cyborgs Are Coming, The Cyborgs Are Coming

There is no doubt that a quantum jump in man's development is in the near future; the Cyborgs are coming, and in turn, will recreate other forms. Evolution is no respector of life. It deals with all life, untold billions. Some survive for a short time, others survive for aeons. Dinosaurs were displaced by forms more advanced, and the process continues. One form surrenders to another, generating new forms of life continually, each more appropriate to the new environment. Our future is evolving in a series of slow progressions made up of quantum jumps similar to the still photos used in time-lapse photography, where various stages of a development are photographed at wide time intervals. As time is compressed, the future is coming toward us at a more rapid rate, and it will leave behind all the earlier forms of life and civilizations that could not make the adjustments. Man will move from the human to the humanoid and then to cybernated organisms. These changes will not be brought about by desire or plan but will be controlled by the forces in the space-time continuum. As our point of view moves from animus, from soul, from spirit, from homonculus, we will come to the realization that man can become like a god through the manipulation of the controls that bind him.

Looking Backward
9   With Futurology

Thousands of articles, books, educational programs, journals, reports, research projects, and organizations are presently devoting much time to a study of the future but few, if any, ponder the possibility of an end to our money system. They are busily forecasting the future of technology, the future of architecture, of women, of urban planning, life styles, energy, genetics, earth sciences, habitats, health and medicine, and hundreds of other areas of interest that merit our serious attention, but their publications leave us with the impression that dollars and cents and trinkets and beads and mazuma and moolah and cabbage and gelt and profit and loss will be here forever. And Republicans and Democrats too.

The Elephant and the Donkey

The *Futurist*, a journal of forecasts and trends published by the World Future Society, presents us with a view of the 1980s as it appears from TRAPS 1, 2, and 5, in a December, 1979, article on the future of our political parties, and gives us some pointers on how we might save the two-party system. The premise of the piece is that the Democrat and Republican parties play a vital role in our system, and should they ever be weakened, democracy itself would crumble. Regard the following: "Once the party system fails to provide a buffer between the government and the special interests, all that is left is a government that is run by and for the special interests."

Party system or no party system, about twenty-five percent of the wealth of the United States is controlled by one percent of its population. These multi-millionaires, who have more money than they or their great-great-grandchildren could ever spend, are the buffer *and* the government as far as influence and public policy is concerned. To devote a whole study (and there are many such well-funded programs) to an analysis of how to "save" the inequitable and antiquated political system that lies at the *bottom of all our problems* says little for the future of futurology.

Futurists should not be talking about saving "politics and business as usual"; if they were aware of the shape of things to come they would be busy drawing up blueprints for the engineering of tomorrow's social system, a system that will assure a fair distribution of goods and services to all of our people. It will be an *engineering* job of enormous magnitude, and it will not be solved by technically-untrained Democrats, Republicans, Socialists, Conservatives, or money-based, politically-oriented, vaguely hypothetical economists, sociologists, and free-enterprisers.

Fossil Power

Rampant power is all around us. A kilowatt of this power is equal to the physical labor of 50 workers, and it costs industry about two cents per hour. It will work forever, 24 hours a day, without vacations, sick leaves, strikes, or lunch breaks. Many American cars are pulled along the highway by the power of 3600 men, and every jet-liner is towed through the friendly skies by power equal to that of almost a million men. If we bother to divide all of the horsepower available in the United States by the number of adults in the population, we would see that our technology has gifted each of us with about 5,000 slaves at his or her disposal.

Futurologists should worry about how we can control all of this raging power. All the political action and advocacy in the world will not alter the fact that it is moving us toward massive social change, where politicians, businessmen, financiers, and other non-technical types will be helpless and unable to contribute to our survival.

The words *control* and *planning* have assumed unfortunate connotations and, because of this, everything is now out of control at the federal, state, county, and city levels. Control is only welcome where it may lead to an increase in profits. But those who oppose the trend toward control and planning are on the losing side because all of this blustering power is hastening the collapse of the money system.

It is astonishing that futurologists do not see that we must discard our bead-and-trinket medium of *exchange* and convert to a medium of *distribution*. It would be easy, in a system controlled by engineers, to clean up the environment and conserve our energy resources. It would be easy to eliminate poverty, debt, lawsuits, welfare, insurance, interest, and taxes; it cannot be done by racial and ethnic movements, business and professional societies, labor organizations, or Democrats and Republicans competing for their share of the spoils.

Poverty is Affluence

Are you interested in contacting extraterrestrial intelligent civilizations? Stop for a moment, and look at the *terrestrial* intelligent civilization all around you. They must be contacted and dealt with immediately; they must be maintained, educated, and entertained. Launching us all into orbit to live in a giant space station is the solution offered by the science fictioneers, but let's call it what it is: at our present state of the art, a fantasy.

Is there a Democrat or Republican who can tell us how to allocate our energy, how to redesign our transportation systems, or how to best distribute all of our productivity? We have never voted on those questions; besides, those problems couldn't be solved in a money system even if anyone knew the answers.

It is interesting to note that not only is our inequity problem not *solvable* by Democrats or Republicans but, ironically, to *try* to solve the problem would threaten many vested interests. Poverty is an industry, a three-billion dollar industry in the United States, and many feed off it: research programs, study groups, expensive consulting organizations, statisticians, computer programmers, and the entire fund-distribution network with its plum administrative jobs.

Just as the threat of international peace affects the economy of whole cities and areas dependent on military contracts, the livelihoods of many thousands depend on the uninterrupted flow of poverty money. For a Congressman to try to offer a solution to defense or poverty spending would be to commit political suicide in these unsane, bereft-of-reason times.

And you wonder why mental illness is on the rise? Mental illness is growing, just as poverty did, into a multi-million dollar industry, and it would be political hara-kiri for anyone to dare suggest a cure for the problem. But there will be one big difference between the poverty industry and the mental illness industry: in poverty, the program is administered by the affluent, in mental illness the administrators will be just as sick as the rest of us.

Nearly all scientists, and some phILOSophers, have the skills, the intelligence, and the scientific approach to solve this enigma. Futurologists, as well, must participate, but they should be forewarned that extrapolations of the future based on studies of our past history cannot help us. The conversion of fossil fuels to 300 kilograms per capita per day is a new phenomenon. There is no historic precedence for the problem of controlling the 20 billion horsepower that we generate daily. Futurologists should also be reminded that Democrats and Republicans were conceived in a hand-tool economy and cannot function in a 20 billion horsepower age.

Computers today are advanced and skillful, but they are doing dumb things. Our technology is clever and well-thought-out, but the game is unsane. In addition, because of a lack of control by technologists, much of our trouble is created by the very technology they have given us: radiation danger from nuclear wastes, toxic food additives, automobile and industrial pollution, and the threat of nuclear war, among others.

Madison Avenue in Orbit

Futurologists, as all of us, are conditioned by the money system and, just as the rest of us, cannot reliably observe the trends of a society of which they are a part. If they could, they would not have endorsed and published the article that appeared in the April, 1979, issue of *The Futurist*, which tells us, from the very bottom of TRAP 1, that "... advertising (faces) revolutionary changes in the years ahead (and) people may be communicating not just with each other but with porpoises, chimpanzees, and extraterrestrial civilizations."

If advertising agencies are the wave of the future, we had all better give up any attempts to better our lives right now. The article goes on to inform us that satellite broadcasting, computers, fiber-optic waveguides, and the videodisc may be used by the purveyors of soap and other sundries, creating new markets in formerly difficult-to-communicate-with areas of the globe. Which is another way of saying that we will be able to dump tons of underarm deodorant into the arms of many deprived third world African nations. At a profit, of course. They assure us, however, that TV commercials may be shortened to a few painless seconds showing nothing more than a company logo and a happy smiling face to establish a connection in the viewer's mind between a specific product and ecstasy. Moreover, with the use of the new technology we may be able to squeeze many commercial messages into a two-minute station break, offering the viewer much more persuasive and important information than we do today.

In the same article, they apprise us of the fact that if telepathic research proves successful, perhaps certain individuals could be taught to communicate telepathically and used as the village scribe or telegrapher were once used. And, of course, no piece on future communications would be complete without re-recounting the story of the metal plaque with the friendly waving couple, Ann and Thro Poe, now riding aboard Pioneer 10. They conclude the article by informing us that the purpose of that message is to enable any intercepting alien race to know when and where the spacecraft originated.

A Million Light-Years Out of Touch

All humans on this planet were raised in a money system, educated in a money system, and taught to use money system language. We are all forced to live with money system values, which teach us that most of our lives should be devoted to competing for money and for what money can buy. Our worth is measured by the thicknesses of our wallets. We are limited in our ability to understand the system by the very fact that we are part of it, and the power of money system conditioning makes it difficult for us to adopt any view other than a money-view toward our fellow humans.

A good example of a money-system-point-of-view is furnished us in a special report by Edward Cornish in the October, 1979, issue of *The Futurist*, which predicts that in the 1980s we will suffer the worst depression in our history. The analysis is comprehensive in its discussion of the many factors that are contributing to the economic down-turn to come: the international monetary crisis, the undercutting of American prices by cheap foreign competition, the influence of the OPEC nations and their U.S. holdings, the lack of liquidity of the average American, the precarious position of the automobile and housing industries, the high cost of production, the energy crisis, rising interest rates, and other contributing factors. But digging through those topographic *symptoms*, we find no single reference to the critical factor responsible: the anachronism of a modern technology operating in an ancient system based on barter.

In a money system operation, the distribution of goods is governed by a system of trade based on a product evaluation which utilizes a medium of exchange made up of debt tokens. Those debt tokens are the very lifeblood of our system; the production and distribution of goods is of secondary importance to the flow of those debt tokens. If that flow is interrupted for any reason, some of the ways used to free it is by the creation of new debt, government subsidy, and increased export, remedies which are at best palliative. The long term cure for debt token stagnation is continuous expansion, which only delays the inevitable, because the debt tokens themselves are the problem.

As a result, what is good for free enterprise is bad for the consumer, and vice versa. But the forces that will force the change to a technologically-planned-and-controlled society are already at work, and what may appear as just another depression in the 1980s is going to be the opening scene of a scenario never experienced by any nation on the planet.

The force of technological productivity and the increasingly high rate of energy conversion per capita per day will be the cause of the demise of the money system. The only way to delay it is to infuse more and more credit into the system which, in three cases, has already been done by war.

The money system conflicts with the laws of physical science. Economic gobbledygook written in money system jargon can never adequately explain what is happening. The reasons given for the coming depression in the *Futurist* article is a million light-years out of touch with reality.

Human Affairs as a Science

If we viewed our enigma as a problem in industrial engineering we would see that money wealth in our system is created by the exercise of debt claims against the physical operation of our production facilities. Real wealth is generated by the conversion of energy in the ground into products and services. The unit of value in our money system is the debt certificate; the unit of value in a system under technological control would be an energy certificate, perhaps rated in ergs, which would have value only during the period it was issued. Bonds and financial debentures could not exist, since they are useless in a technological operation of this kind.

The technologically-controlled-society-to-come will operate with the same scientific method used up to now to produce all the technological wonders of our modern world, including the Viking landing on Mars and the space colonies to come. Any scientist studying our system would soon discover that it is a system of exchanging goods and services for money. That same scientist, if asked to design a more efficient operation, would propose a non-money system which would distribute goods and services by a computerized accounting technique utilizing some sort of energy certificate. And each citizen would receive a fair share of the total wealth.

Our present system can best be described as schizoid: it uses scientific methods to produce goods, then exchanges these goods under a primitive exchange system utilizing beads and trinkets, the value and fluctuations of which has never been clearly understood by anyone.

The direction of the trend is obvious to anyone who would forget "economics" and approach it as a systems problem. It would be clear to futurologists too, if they would stop trying to explain an engineering problem with the cliches of economics. America has designed and built the most complex array of technological equipment on this planet. It has the highest number of skilled personnel and the highest consumption of extraneous energy per capita that ever existed. Production trends indicate that, contrary to the analyses of economists, we will soon reach a maximum product level that will be limited by the capacity of our population to consume. There is no way of reversing this trend.

Since every trend has a limit, as we approach this limit we will be forced to install a social organization capable of operating our society. Such an operation will give birth to the lowest amount of human labor per capita and the highest standard of living this planet has ever seen.

It would be naive to think that a new social system would be welcomed by the financial and political interests that control our economy; kings-of-the-hill use every possible method to maintain their position. They have managed so far to keep themselves on top of the hill by deficit spending, war, and welfare, and have convinced most of us, including the futurologists, that all has been well.

We are all aware of what is wrong but it would not hurt us to list some of these as triggers: the soaring prices of homes, cost of living, medical and dental costs, hospital costs; work lay-offs, rising crime rates, sabotage, terrorism, unfair employment practices, racial and sexual discrimination, civil rights violations, small brush fire wars, exploitation of sex and violence, the torpor of television and movies, corruption in big business and high places, misrepresentation in advertising, pollution — all caused by the money system.

When will scientists look up from their microscopes and down from their telescopes, and see that our whole system would come to a grinding halt without them, that only they can solve our social problems, and that our one hope for tomorrow is the establishment of a science of human affairs today?

Monkeys are
10   People Too

The behavior of electrons, the phenomenon of gravitation, the nuclear fireball that makes up our sun and the uncountable number of other suns — the very nature of the world, from the smallest particle we can measure, to the trackless distances of the universe that we can probe — all that we have observed and measured, including our own planet and the organisms that exist in the oceans, on the land, and in the gaseous envelope around us, all of this is the world as we know it. In all this world, our observations have never uncovered any material or process existing separately, independently isolated, and uniquely obeying its own special set of laws. Yet many scientists, especially the proponents of the idea that "technologically advanced intelligent civilizations" may exist on some other planet, continue to imply that the part of the universe that is enclosed within the body of a human is somehow apart and different, as it stands outside the world and studies it with a mysterious mind that is exempt from the laws that govern all else.

We all know today that the earth and the sun and the planets do not possess free will as the ancients once believed. Any schoolboy can tell us that their motion is dependent on forces. A ripe apple falls from a tree not because it desires to reach the ground, as some ancient philosophers believed but, as we know now, because of the force of gravity. The leaves of plants and trees do not turn toward the sun because they are intelligently purposeful but, as we know now, because of the phenomenon of phototropism, which is the effect of the bombardment of light energy on the plant's chemistry and structure. All organisms that inhabit the earth are part of the world, and their existence and behavior are dependent on the many independent variables that control them.

Man is not exempt from this control. He is not guided through life by a little man inside of him peeking out through his eyes. He does not behave because of his desires; if he did, he would then be immune to all the laws of the universe, like the apple which falls not because of gravity but because it desires to reach the ground. This is a difficult idea to grasp because everything we have been taught runs counter to it.

Any shape and arrangement of organism that we can imagine has at one time been presented to the world, which then selects only those it can support. The process is one of editing rather than authorship. In an article in the *New Yorker* of April 16, 1966, George Wald of Harvard says: "This is the way organic design works. It is design by hindsight rather than foresight. In that sense it is just the opposite of technological design. Technological design works by setting specifications and trying to achieve them. Organic design works by continuous selection among random variations."

Dr. Wald is on the right track, but when he says that technological design is different from the selective process, he hasn't taken the selection idea far enough. The specifications that technologists set can only be established by hindsight, just as in nature. *Technological progress is a result of discovery by empirical testing.* Man does not invent; all of his artifacts are the result of discovery, or accident, after which he may then set down specifications. Biologically speaking, there is no such phenomenon as creativity, unless one believes in magic.

Dr. Wald also uses the word *random*. *Random can only be a pattern we do not understand*. When we drop a handful of steel balls to the floor, they fall, roll to a stop, and arrange themselves in what we call a random pattern, but we know that the final resting place of each ball is predictable if we are aware of all the forces and collisions involved, a process similar to "predicting" the weather. The shapes, sizes, and arrangements of organisms — the mutations — are the result of forces such as cosmic radiation, heat, and exposure to certain chemicals. There is a reason for all occurrences in nature, nothing is random, all is lawful, Man's anatomy and physiology happens as a result of external forces, and it is then accepted or rejected by the environment. He is part of the world and continually controlled by it.

This process of selection by the environment also applies to his behavior, or what we call his personality. A person is a repertoire of behaviors selected by his environment out of the many bits of behavior that he has emitted in his lifetime.

Years ago many scientists believed that life was the result of spontaneous generation. Louis Pasteur then demonstrated that the chemical fermentation of buttermilk or beer was caused by minute organisms present in the atmosphere and not spontaneously generated in the liquid. Lord Lister revolutionized surgical practice by using carbolic acid to prevent atmospheric germs from putrifying the healing of compound fractures.

Today the spontaneous generation theory is considered absurd, but the idea of the spontaneous generation of behavior is still widely held. The uses of such terms as *self-motivation*, *intent*, *will*, imply a kind of autonomous spontaneously-driven human who moves about capriciously with his decision-making brain at the helm steering him through life, somehow exempt from the forces and laws of the universe.

Let us look again at the idea of inventing a mind to explain the behavior of organisms. Green plants turn their leaves toward the sun because of phototropism. If we could watch phototropism at work we would clearly see why plants are forced to turn. As complex as they are, we know that plant movements are not more than an electro-physico-chemical (we could hyphenate forever) phenomenon. If the foregoing is true of plants, why shouldn't it be true for all other forms of life?

A Design for Living

The animals we see around us, including ourselves, are those whom the environment is able to support. Many billions of different forms of life have been exposed to the environment in the past. Those of which we know are the ones that have survived such exposure; that the environment was able to support. Sudden changes in the species, quantum jumps, a series of "accidents" properly called mutations, are continually offered up to a selection committee (the world around us) for a decision on whether they live or die. The selection committee includes such members as the pressure and chemistry of the ocean and air on the earth's surface, the supportive nature of other plants and animals, planet temperature, solar and cosmic radiation, gravity, and more.

But how can living forms be so well designed to perform the daily tasks of everyday living if there is no engineering or planning involved? We said it before, but we will re-state the answer to that question: we do not have arms *in order* to perform manual tasks — we perform manual tasks *because* we have arms. What we do is determined by what we have. We do not have eyes *in order* to see, we see *because* we have eyes. There are many things we do not do because we do not have the equipment. For example, if we had an eye in the back of our heads or a third arm projecting from our chests we could perform many other tasks. It would then appear that the extra eye or third arm were designed to perform in such a manner, rather than the other way around.

Organisms are not *designed* for a *purpose*. The word *purpose* has no meaning in an intelligent discussion, and the word *design* has no meaning in the sense that it is ordinarily used. The nature of the design process in the universe is one of selection. The word *invention*, which presupposes purpose, also has no meaning. Animals, including humans, *discover*, not *invent*. The process of invention is "cut and try", or empirical. We load a column with a series of weights to determine at what point it will collapse. Its collapse point cannot be predicted, computed, or calculated unless tried first. We can then say, or predict, on the basis of past exposure to test experience, that columns twice as thick will perhaps buckle under twice the load, and so forth.

Bridges weren't invented. A tree once fell across a stream after a lightning storm and it was *discovered* that one's feet didn't get wet when crossing the stream by way of the felled tree. There was one trouble with this bridge, it blocked water traffic. After many years, someone *discovered* that he could paddle his canoe under a raised portion of the tree. This discovery led to the use of high bridges, in order to clear the lane for water traffic.

Man first built a rigid glider after watching the flight of birds for aeons. He then *discovered*, through a series of empirical tries called *tests*, that a propeller or airscrew, which was already in use on ships, would be easier to drive and more efficient than birdlike flapping wings. When lighter and stronger materials became available through the process of discovery, and only after the internal combustion engine was developed by the same process, a large "bird" was built with a propeller driven by a gasoline engine. It was crude, and the first flight was of short duration and slow. But through the years the design process of *cut and try* gradually shaped the configuration of this bird to look like what it does today. Engines became more powerful and lighter, structural materials became lighter and stronger, and the aerodynamic configuration was literally shaped in wind tunnel research. Wind tunnels are used for blowing air at high speed at various shaped models of wings and bodies. Instead of moving the models through the air, we blow air past the models and discover which shapes are less resistant to the air (move faster) at the least cost of energy, and where to locate and how to shape our control surfaces for optimum efficiency. A simple definition of efficiency: *the most for the least* or *the most work for the least energy.*

All processes, products, and organisms, including man and his artifacts, are selected, shaped, and honed by their interaction with the world, which is also shaped in the same way. We see now that we may use the word *design* in a new sense while we discard our old use of the term, so that we can move forward in our view of the world.

A difficult concept to grasp (and it will continue to elude us even when we think we have it) is the fact that organisms continuously behave under the control of their environment, that their behavior is not generated and controlled by an inner mind or will. Difficult to grasp or not, it is so, and if we want to advance in our understanding of the life processes we must accept that underlying truth. One reason why it is difficult to grasp is that everything we have learned, everything we have recorded in our history of mankind, everything we read in our daily papers seems to contradict that truth. And virtually all anthropologists and psychologists continue to describe the behavior of humans and human society in language that should have been discarded years ago.

A tree is a dependent variable whose changes are linked to the changes in other independent variables. A tree, like us, is made up of tangible, measurable, physical materials and processes (the word *physical* should be unnecessary in a scientific discussion. To talk about anything other than physical is to talk about nothing). A monkey, while more complex, lives in the same world as the tree and is subject to the same laws. There is nothing special or unique about a monkey in the sense that he may be other than a physical process; like us, he is made up of tangible, measurable, physical materials and processes, and his behavior is a function of other controlling variables. Monkeys are people too.

Any life form that we can imagine or draw with pencil and paper has probably surfaced at one time in the past 3 to 5 billion years. What we are looking at when we look at a baby is an anatomy, a physiology, and a behavior which is the result of billions of years of selection by the environment. And babies throughout the world are generally the same, aside from slight physiological differences such as pigmentation, features, and stature.

TRAP 2 Revisited

There is a popular game played at outdoor drive-in movies. After sunset has darkened the sky, but before the movie begins, restless patrons will point the spotlights attached to their cars at the movie screen. A chase usually ensues, with one light spot chasing another. Some perform weird "dances" as their owners guide them through eccentric patterns. While watching the display it is difficult not to think of the spots of light as human. Although we know they are only moving spots of illumination, we tend to assign human qualities to them, with the light spots acquiring the characteristics of "cute personalities".

The same phenomenon takes place when we observe an industrial machine performing a complex operation. In a bottling plant one can observe "clever" steel fingers lift bottles, rinse them, and pass them to a dryer, which then lines them up on a conveyor belt, where they are shunted downstream to fill-spouts before they are capped and labeled. After this, they are arranged neatly into cases which are sealed and stacked, ready to be mounted on a truck for delivery. Computers appear to be "intelligent" humans in their calculating, storage, and retrieval operations, because they remind us of humans. We should not be criticized if we sometimes respond to them emotionally.

Soon we will have voice-operated switches and machine operations which will perform at our command. Let's call them electronic slaves. But for now, we are not interested in the marvels of technology as much as we are interested in the behavioral tendency to assign human qualities to them and respond to them as if they were human. It is obvious that if we wish to understand how computers and automated technology work we would be wasting our time if we searched for a mind, or a soul, or a personality, or motivation. The only useful approach to understanding, and eventually controlling and improving such machinery would be an approach based on the scientific method; some measuring technique utilizing our most advanced analytic instruments. It would also help us to know that the machine we are analyzing is just a machine made up of tangible, real, hardware, and *nothing else*. Our task becomes easier when we realize too that all the machine's functions and processes are lawful, meaning that it moves and works for physical and measurable reasons.

Consider: If it is true about machines, and if it is true about physics, chemistry and astronomy, it is also true about everything else in the universe. All phenomena, whether they are the movement of planets or the behavior of organisms, are real, material, and capable of being analyzed and controlled, because in the universe everything is law-abiding.

Where humans are concerned, we are more apt to understand them if we approach them as mechanisms; we can be more helpful (more humane) if we adopt this approach. In whose hands would you be safer: a warm, emotional, human surgeon or a skilled, technically-competent surgeon who cared not one whit about you as a person but was dedicated to skillfully solving a functional problem? The captain of a modern jet-liner had better be a technical man placed there for his ability, rather than elected by the popular vote of the passengers. It turns out that the person who really possesses humanity, compassion, and rachmuness is the "cold" person who can do something to make our lives healthier and happier; pity, compassion, and humanity are hollow words if used in any other context. What appears to be "cold" materialistic science is in reality all the humanism we all need.

Let us return to the idea of erroneously projecting human-ness into machines and organisms. Any computer-scientist who talked about the soul of computers would be revealing his ignorance, even to the non-scientific person. Yet this is what the phILOSophers do when they talk about communicating (in human terms) with a non-human world. The term "communication" does not apply even to our own planet because it is fallacious, in the same sense that it is fallacious to think that a computer has a soul. The error of the phILOSophers is that they invariably apply erroneous earth-terms to space phenomena, erroneous because they are vitalistic, or animistic. The most valuable discovery we shall make in our search for "life" is what we will discover about ourselves. We shall learn that we have been looking for something that is not there, like looking for the soul in a computer.

It is an interesting irony that machines are not like humans and humans are not like the machines to which we compare them. We err in both directions. The computer analogy, with its terms like *control, processing, storage* and *retrieval*, does not apply to the human brain. To speak of our brains as intelligent computers is to see it backwards. We do not deduce, or think, or know, anything — the world is continually acting on us. The brain does perform an important function, but it does not initiate or control behavior; it mediates behavior between the stimulus and the response.

To control specific behavior in a human (to cause a person to rise from a chair, walk a mile, then drink a glass of water) it is necessary to manipulate the environment. A human drinks water because he is deprived of it, not because he is thirsty; to say he drinks because he is thirsty is to explain nothing. To say that he searches his memory (the storage metaphor) for a forgotten name is to say that he has another eye inside of his head, and that he knows what he is looking for. If he knows the name he is looking for, if he can recognize it when he locates it in his memory storage bank, then he must already know the name. On the other hand, if he has "forgotten" the name (doesn't know it), how will he recognize it when he finds it?

We seem to be talking about a little man inside of our heads who is frantically operating our internal computer, making decisions, thinking constructively, creating great works of art, inventing machines, uncovering the laws of science, probing the secrets of the universe, contemplating himself as Dr. Wald does in Chapter Two, and so forth. These are the phrases used by the phILOSophers. And they are more than phrases; they are the kind of errors that prevent us from taking the next giant step in science. We are part of the space-time continuum, a link in an infinite time-and-space-chain in an infinitely dense universe, which is at the same time a void.

Explanation stops at this point.

Communicating With
11   Words and Pictures

In physics, scientists are concerned with activity. One might ask: "What about structure?" But when we analyze it a little further, scientists are concerned with the structure of activity. The only evidence we have of any phenomenon in nature is its activity, or behavior, whether it be its effect on other phenomena or material, or itself. The sun is the sun because of its activity. We are aware of it because of its activity. The only evidence we have of it is its behavior as a sun. *Intelligence* can only mean activity. The only evidence we have of intelligence is the behavior from which it is inferred.

We must think in terms of *process*. Intelligence, the behavior that we call *intelligence*, is part of this vast process that is continually taking place in nature. What does one know when one acquires knowledge? Certainly there is a change in behavior with respect to the environment. Scientists behave differently from non-scientists; scientific laws are actually codified forms of behavior. For example, scientists cannot "know" why material falls toward the earth. When they tell us it is obeying the laws of gravity, they are modulating their behavior with respect to the phenomenon. As the environment shapes a man's behavior it shapes his ability to "control" his environment, but the environment remains always in dominant control. We, the products of nature, depend on the forces and elements of the universe to sustain us, and our behavior is no exception to this rule. When we become aware of this, we can begin to understand that intelligent life on earth is not intelligent, and that communication is not what it appears to be.

What Will They Be Like?

Realizing, as even the phILOSophers do, that other life forms in outer space would appear biologically different from us, we must try to visualize what kind of a "civilization" could exist on another planet. First let us imagine a situation on Earth, as we observe a group of humans interrelating with each other in a foreign language. The entire situation would appear mysterious, although slightly understandable, as many of the things that they do would be recognizable since we are culturally almost identical. We could sense that some of the words between them were questions, some were answers, some were approvals, and some were not.

But now picture a group of humans, this time English-speaking ones, under a large dome of soundproof glass, while we remain outside looking in. Their behavior would appear more mysterious than the behavior of the foreigners. We would see a lot of dashing about, a lot of what formerly we knew as conversation but now not meaning much to us as we watch them reacting angrily or happily to each other, approving of each other, disapproving, engaging in wars for strange reasons, etc. The same phenomenon can be experienced while watching a motion picture film with the sound off, or a television program with the volume lowered to inaudible. But even in these cases, we would be familiar with the surroundings. They would be sitting in familiar chairs, driving familiar automobiles, and indulging in scientific research with familiar instrumentation. Even if the artifacts were not familiar, the humans themselves would be — their legs, their arms, their physical and behavioral configuration would have some meaning to us.

Let us now picture different organisms — different shapes, different color, different means of locomotion — living in a strange environment and interacting with each other. Let us look at some of their scientists. We would notice, as a result of their "research", an alteration of the environment, or a "technology" as the phILOSophers would call it. Now we have another picture: strange globs moving about in a strange world, with strange artifacts, in a completely senseless manner, If we were perceptive, we would realize that all of the activity was caused, created, and controlled by its surroundings. Planets "know" about the universe because they are part of it. Two trees standing ten-feet apart know of each other's presence; if one tree is felled, the other one knows it because there is a disturbance to the air between them.

Planets know about the universe, but can they communicate this to us? We, being part of the universe, also "know". The word *communication* is as misleading as the word *intelligence*, because there is no way to communicate with these other "life forms" on other planets. We could just as easily communicate with the earth and ask it questions about the origin of the universe. Strictly speaking, even on the surface of the earth, within the same language and culture, there is no communication taking place between individuals, if by *communication* we mean idea transmission. Words and sounds affect other humans in a behavioral way. When we understand this concept, we then understand the fallacy, and the danger, of using terms as *communication* and *intelligence*.

There cannot be an intelligent civilization on another planet for the same reason that there isn't one here. We "learn"only through interaction with the environment. As we noted earlier, there is no such phenomenon as creativity or invention; all is discovery, and it happens "randomly".

And there is no such phenomenon as randomness, in the sense that its behavior is unlawful; there is a law to explain all behavior in the universe.

The attitude of the phILOSophers is the attitude of little boys overwhelmed with a science-fiction view of the future. Space travel will come, we will know the surfaces and the activities of other planets, and eventually other solar systems and galaxies. We will become cognizant of what appears now to be a state of nothingness, but is infinitely dense with material. Eventually, as our instruments become more refined, we will see more and more of the universe around us right here on the surface of the earth in what appears to be a void, but is in reality filled with fast-moving particles.

The goal of science should be the well-being of man, and that is where we are going: to a longer life of well-being. We could try to communicate with other life forms on earth, if we must amuse ourselves, but it will never work. If it appears to work, what will be happening is that we are simply learning to affect the behavior of other life forms through conditioning, and other techniques. Try communicating with an armadillo. You say he knows nothing, he does not possess an advanced technology? Neither do we — let's not flatter ourselves. With all our "knowledge", we are simply creating minor scratches on the surface of a floating piece of debris in the solar system. Yes, one day we will leave it, but we will leave as an explosion of the planet Earth and not under the control of our "will", "intent", "desire", or "motivation".

This text makes use of many archaic terms because the English language does not supply us with more convenient tools. Since it is impossible to talk about a language with that same language, we are forced to commit the sin while discussing it. Note how the language tricks us: anything is possible. If anything is possible, why not intelligent civilizations on other planets? Wrong language. For instance, anything is possible but, as we stated before, it is not possible to make an automobile fly. If we can make an automobile fly, it is no longer an automobile, because it requires modification of some sort. Some things are not possible because the language we use to describe it is invalid. The word *automobile* means a vehicle that rolls on the ground. We are therefore asked to make a vehicle that rolls on the ground not roll on the ground. The problem is one of definition, and leads to the kind of trouble in which the phILOSophers are deeply mired.

Accents, Languages, and Values

Assuming that they did exist, there are many reasons why we could not possibly communicate with alien life forms who have other values, cultures, biologies, and interests. Let us explore this aspect. There is no place in the world, outside of New York City, where people speak with a New York accent, because the New York accent is a product of a specific environment. The reason that this environmental control is not repeated anywhere else is the same reason that there are no two snowflakes with the same design. We might say that since there are billions and billions of snowflakes falling on the Earth during a heavy snowstorm there must be two snowflakes with the same design, but there aren't. In an infinity there is also an infinity of differences.

The phILOSophers say that since the universe is vast, that somewhere in that vastness there must be another planet similar to ours. But like the grains of sand on a beach, there are no two grains that look alike; there is an infinity of differences. For that reason it is impossible to find another area on Earth whose people speak English with a New York accent. The reason we stress this point is to shed light on the fact that people's cultures, languages, attitudes, and behaviors differ even within the same species.

Chinese people speak a different language and have a different set of values than Norwegians, although these differences are rapidly disappearing. There is a strong tendency toward uniformity because of the airplane, radio, television, and publication. It wasn't too many years ago that in the United States, in the North and the South, the East and the West, one would encounter different diets, costumes, and also pronounced differences in accents. But today, because of the motion picture and television, people are beginning to speak alike, dress alike, and eat the same foods.

Different environments produce different people, and the differences lie in their behavior, their speech, their language, their costumes, their diets, and the many other details that relate to lifestyle. The airplane is rapidly evening out the differences in the United States. The products of one environment are flying into other environments — Northerners fly to the South, and Southerners fly to the North. The motion picture is spreading speech patterns, and there is a somewhat standard American English used by network radio and television announcers and newscasters.

Radio and television have assumed speech control over localities, slowly wiping out regionalisms and localisms. The New York dialect is still not to be found in Paris, or in Chicago, or San Francisco, although the San Francisco dialect somewhat resembles the New York because harbors are touched by ships which spread speech patterns rapidly. For that reason, there is a similarity in the speech of a native San Franciscan, a New Yorker, and a native of New Orleans.

In the United States there still exists a Southern dialect, a New York accent, and the Chicago speech. There is also a California speech, especially in the Los Angeles area, which is close to the American standard. And there are little pockets that have their own peculiarities like the Piedmont in West Virginia, the Boston accent, the special flavor of Minneapolis, Minnesota, and the Pittsburgh speech in western Pennsylvania, where the rising inflection of a question is a little different from the rest of the country.

We encounter more major differences when we move, not from accent to accent, but from language to language — say from English to French. There is even more difference encountered when we compare English with Russian, or when we compare Chinese with Bantu, or Spanish with Arabic, although there is a spillover of Arabic terms into the Spanish language since the invasion of the Moors. For a member of one language culture to try to communicate with a member of another language culture, utilizing only speech, is to attempt an impossible task. There is no way that a Chinese could communicate any information to an English-speaking person. Another point we must remember is that the life expectancy of the languages of our planet are not fixed and constant, but dynamically variable, along with meaning and semantic implication. Man's history is littered with the detritus of hundreds of languages that have vanished such as Hittite, Cuneiform, Babylonian, Egyptian, Phoenician, Rongo Rongo, Mycenean, Etruscan, and many others, including scores of Amer-Indian ones, not to mention classical Greek and Latin. And today, although English has become the *lingua franca* of the world, we are left with a variety of languages which differ widely from each other, like Arabic, Hindustani, Mandarin Chinese, Greek, Polish, German, Swahili, Russian, and Portuguese.

Self-Consciousness, Awareness and Ego

Let us move beyond language differences and see what happens when we try to communicate with another species, from man to zebra, or from man to elephant, or even from man to dog, his best friend. It is not possible for man to communicate with a dog, although it appears so when we observe a dog respond to conditioned word cues, which is something else.

Now what happens when we attempt communication with another life form that is neither mammal nor fish — a plant, for instance? With whatever speech pattern or code we may devise, we cannot communicate with a plant nor a plant with us, using the term *communication* in the commonly accepted sense. If we accept the fact that the only communication possible on planet Earth is between members of the same language culture, we must stop and examine that also. Upon analysis, what appears to be communication is really word conditioning. People are conditioned by each other, by society, by their parents, by other factors influential in their early training, to respond in specific ways to specific word patterns and sounds. When a speaker utters words to a listener he is emitting a behavior which elicits another behavior from the listener and from himself.

The process is fundamentally a behavioral phenomenon. One organism does something, the other organism (the listener) does something in response to the something that the speaker does, and as a result, there is a new combination of behaviors in the speaker-listener relationship. The sentence "Get me my hat, please" is a behavior that the speaker knows from his past will produce his hat. The listener, who has heard this request in the past, will respond as he has been conditioned to respond to that behavior and produce the hat. The phenomenon of communication also takes place with the speaker as his own listener; and that is what we call *thinking*. When the speaker becomes conscious of self, in reality he is speaking to himself as a listener, and responding as a listener to himself, the speaker. What takes place between two organisms can also take place *within* an organism, and this is what we call self consciousness, awareness, or ego. If there were no speech, there would be no "awareness".

To summarize, it is easy for two New Yorkers to communicate with each other. It is a little more difficult for a New Yorker and a Southerner to communicate with each other. It is extremely difficult, if not impossible, for a Russian speaking Russian and a New Yorker speaking English to communicate with each other. It becomes more difficult for a member of one species to communicate with a member of another species. Man cannot talk to a dog, and a dog cannot communicate with man. What appears to be communication within the same language group is a form of behavior; individuals bouncing about in a conditioned response to sounds emitted by each other. For the most part, thinking is sub-vocalization — speaking to oneself — or as some modern experimental psychologists call it, covert speech, speech not heard by another. We can say now that what appears to be communication is not.

What About Pictures?

Since it is impossible for members of different language groups to communicate with each other, it is more impossible, if we may use that expression, for a member of this planet to communicate with a so-called alien of another planets with words, or any other language. We might ask, "What about pictures? Why couldn't we use pictures to communicate with alien beings on another planet?" Let us assume that their biology is similar to ours — that they have a sense of vision, and can understand perspective drawings projected on a flat surface, or holographic representations. What is a picture? What is seeing? What does a person see when he sees, how does seeing occur, and why do different people looking at the same object see differently?

Many years ago, when photography was discovered, people reproduced on a flat plate a crude, but somewhat realistic, representation of an object, created by the effect of light on a photosensitive surface. Years later, the quality, the contrast, the greys, and the values improved. The picture became a more realistic representation of objects and space. The next milestone was the arrival of motion pictures. We were now able to record the dynamics of an object in motion, and *capture the past*. A motion picture of leaves swaying in the wind last week, shown on a screen today, is displaying a captured representation of what happened last week exactly as it occurred.

Then came color, and after that three-dimensional motion pictures, although it is still far from perfect and requires the use of peripheral aids such as special glasses. We are rapidly moving in the direction of three-dimensional photography; if you wish to call it photography you may, but it will actually be a representation of solid objects in space. Holography will give us a picture that we will be able to walk around and view as a solid object projected in space. Television now enables us to instantly communicate a picture in color, to another location many miles away. Soon, and it is inevitable, we will have three-dimensional television, a kind of instant communicable holography, and then, a speech by the President of the United States* could actually be a visit to your home, where he will sit in a chair and address you quietly rather than in loud stentorian tones.

Soon we will have video communication by telephone, with the help of satellites, which will reduce the need to travel. A money system salesman*, rather than fly to Chicago from Los Angeles to show samples, will simply dial and show his wares, showing various colors, and various styles.

We are now at the point of three-dimensional color repre-

*These are only examples. It is hoped that the money system, with its politicians and salesmen, will be long gone by then.

sentation of objects. The next step will be to transmit it through the television and telephone, and the step beyond that will be to move from what appears to be a projection to a solid reality, a picture that we could actually touch, hold, turn, and squeeze. You say, "Impossible." It is not only possible, it is happening; it is in the process of happening, and *will* happen as technological development accelerates, faster and faster, into the future. A picture, as we know it today, is a step in the development of the capturing of reality.

We Must Know to See

What is *seeing?* There is a powerful "psychological" component involved in seeing. One must *learn* to see. An artist or a poet looking at a complex automobile engine will see a general haze. An automobile engineer looking at the same engine will see something different. The automobile engineer, who understands the relationship and purpose of every part at which he looks, is seeing something totally different from what the poet is seeing. Yes, they are both aware of a mass of metal, and if necessary the poet could avoid rather than collide with it if he were walking across the floor, but in order to see as we would like to use the term, he would have to *know.* A poet looking at a bridge does not see what a structural engineer sees in a bridge. To see well is to know well, and to know well is to see well.

Correct seeing also relates to health. A person who sees honestly, structurally, scientifically, and objectively is not affected by what he sees, in the sense that he is not emotionally moved or damaged by the event that he is viewing. A psychiatrist walking through a group of emotionally disturbed individuals looks at the situation with a clinical eye; an untrained layman is affected by it. Awareness is an essential component of seeing, and it allows us to be untouched and unaffected by what we see.

If it takes such highly-specialized training to see objects properly, objectively, structurally, and with understanding, as we have demonstrated in the example of the poet and the engineer looking at an engine, we must realize that attempting to communicate visually or graphically with organisms even on this Earth is a difficult process, fraught with distortion. Then how can one communicate with alien beings on another planet, utilizing pictures? The term *communication* is used widely and quite loosely by the phILOSophers, with little thought, anthropomorphically, and quite chauvinistically, to use their own language.

Let us restate: what we see as a communication of ideas between organisms is a visual-acoustic phenomenon that is part of a complex behavior pattern. There is no *idea transmission*. To use the computer analogy or to use analogies from the field of information theory and communication is fallacious. There is no data being transmitted; neither is there evidence of storage in the brain — of messages, words, pictures, or graphics of any kind. If we looked into a skull we would see nothing but bone, tissue, muscle, nerve, and blood. These do represent something, but they represent activity. What happens when a man learns something new is that his behavior changes and he becomes another person; if we understand this, we must reject the idea of communicating with other species on other planets. Note that we have disregarded the techniques of writing, printing, and hieroglyphics, which are fundamentally the annotation of speech sounds. For the purpose of this book we shall think of writing and all forms of written speech as acoustic speech. Writing is to language what piano sheet music is to piano sound.

Life is a Projection

Not only does communication not exist as the phILOSophers envision it, but neither does life. There is a kind of chauvinism involved in their use of the term, because when we look at a man and see a man we are projecting "man-ness" into him. What we should see if we looked at a man clinically, scientifically, objectively, without value judgement, without feeling, without emotion, without involvement, and without projection, is a machine. A smile shouldn't be symbolic of anything. A word should mean nothing to us; neither should a look of the eye, an expression, a frown, a posture, or a behavior. We should look at a man as we look at a machine to see him *correctly*. (Allow us to use the term *correctly* because there is no word in the English language to correctly express what we mean.)

Assuming an Intention

There is an old experiment in psychology labelled "intentionality assumption". A movie was shown to a group of people. The first scene was simply a square with a triangle alongside it. The audience was simply seeing the outline of a square, with the outline of a triangle alongside of it. But then the triangle began to move toward the square. Now the audience was seeing a square being approached by a triangle, but the audience was still not involving themselves in any externalizing. Then the square moved away from the triangle and the triangle pursued the square. When the square went up the triangle went up, when the square went down the triangle went down. Now the audience was amused and saw something else. They began to project animism into what was simply a picture of a square and a triangle moving in relation to each other, and they began to see them as people.

The triangle leaped upon the square, and the square eluded the triangle. The square leaped upon the triangle, and what followed was a "battle" between the square and the triangle. By now the audience was watching two characters engaged in conflict, yet we know that they were not characters. One was a square and the other was a triangle, and they were moving on the screen, and there was no meaning and no significance intended except that which was projected into the scene by the audience. That is what takes place when one looks at an organism that appears to be "cute", say a squealing mouse, a purring kitten, or a bunny rabbit. The "cuteness" is projected into the organism by the viewer, just as that audience projected "life" into the square - triangle relationship.

Organisms are really only squares or triangles; with arms, legs, eyes, ears, movement, pose, structure, and noise, All else is added by the viewer. That is an important point — *what appears to be life is a projection by the viewer.* A skilled surgeon performing his work is not looking at a human, he is working on a malfunctioning mechanism and correcting an abnormality. The phILOSophers are chauvinistically seeing life in what isn't, and thinking in "life" terms of living organisms inhabiting other planets. When they use the term *advanced technological civilization* they are projecting our cultural values into another group. We may, of course, find movement on the surface of other planets; complex material organizations may be moving on, under, or even above the surface of an alien planet. But we should not use the term "organism" because that implies animism, a life that we are projecting into what is basically material, just as the audience did in the square - triangle experiment, although these material organizations may be dashing about on the surface of another planet emitting squeaks and squeals of all sorts and bouncing about in such a manner that would easily tempt us to label them as *living*, just as we did with the square and the triangle.

A motion picture camera does not see life when it photographs behaving organisms. It is we who see life when we see the projection of this photography on a motion picture screen.* Similar to the case of the square and the triangle, when one observes three or four ants crawling about on a table, a massive example of projection takes place. We are seeing what we term *aggressiveness, intent, purpose, fear, sexual drive, hunger drive, motivation,* and everything else not there. This is why the approach to the study of behavior by the modern radical behaviorists is on the right track — they are looking for environmental clues, the basic mechanisms that drive, propel, and shape the behavior of organisms.

Is Man Exempt from the Laws of the Universe?

A fundamental idea, unsaid, but nevertheless clearly at the bottom of all statements by the phILOSophers, is that we are looking out at the universe. We are about to explore it, we will begin to understand it, we will search through the galaxies, and we will find other civilizations which may tell us what they know about the universe and its beginnings, and we shall then share all these wonderful secrets about *that universe out there.* They tend to see the universe as made up of two parts: a universe, and we scientists observing that universe. They do not see, as they should, a single universe of which we are a part. *We cannot know the universe because we are part of the universe.* We cannot know that of which we are a part. There is no such phenomenon as *knowing* — basically, physically, structurally speaking; we are at best only part of the infinite space-time continuum.

There are no people out there. There are no people on planet Earth. There are organisms who are the products of a millenium of development on the surface of the earth, in the

---

*A pellucid way to put it: A projector projects an image of a man on the screen and we project an image of life into him.

oceans, and in the air. The birds, the animals, and all that moves on, under, about, and above the earth are part of the behavior of the planet and the universe, and are driven and controlled by forces outside of them. There is no animism, there is no soul, there is no homunculus, there is no golem, there is no dybbuk, there is no ghost, there is nothing that should or could be exorcised out of a human being. An old story is told to prove the existence of a soul: the supporters of the soul idea used to say that when a man died he weighed less because his soul left him, and that was proof that there was a soul. But they always explained that the soul was spiritual, was not material, was a kind of nothing. Well, if it was nothing and not material, how could the man weigh less? In order for him to weigh less, a mass had to leave him. Therefore the soul was made up of something.

Infinitely Dense and Infinitely Empty

There is no *nothing*. Everything has to be made up of stuff: tangible, real, massive stuff. Energy is mass. Energy cannot be nothing. Light is not nothing; light is made up of particles of *stuff*, of tangible, one-day-measurable, stuff. When we speak of space we tend to imply a nothingness between two solid objects, but if there was nothing between the earth and the Moon it would take us no time to get there. Space is infinitely solid but not to *our* senses. If, as we stated before, a fast-moving motion picture camera, one that moved at five billion frames-per-second, was aimed at what appeared to be empty space, it might pick up giant globs of matter moving at tremendous rates of speed in all directions. You say, how can giant globs of matter be moving through what appears to be empty space? Wouldn't they destroy us if they passed through us? That would be a violation of the law of physics. But there is another law that prevails.

A rock thrown at a sheet of glass would cause the sheet of glass to shatter into many pieces. A stone thrown swiftly at a sheet of glass would create a hole, with some splintering around the hole. A bullet fired through a sheet of glass would create an almost clean hole. A very fast moving bullet fired through a sheet of glass would create what would appear to the human eye as a finely honed, sharp, splinterless hole. The faster the speed, the less damage. Straws blown in the wind during a hurricane have been known to penetrate the trunks of trees to a depth of six inches. Try pushing a straw through the trunk of a tree by hand.

Light particles shining through glass appear to do no damage, we do not see any holes as a result. There is some damage, but we do not see any holes as a result. Yes, there is some damage, but certainly not evident to us. X-ray and cosmic radiation move through solid masses of metal without damaging them. There is some damage taking place, but it is not very evident. When radiation moves through an object it is occupying the same space, in a sense, at the same time as the object itself. So with high speed concepts, velocity, acceleration, and time fall into a strange realm of physics where none of the old laws apply. If we fired a fast moving one-foot diameter steel sphere through the air at a "tremendous" speed, it would probably do no damage to an organism standing in its way. That is almost an impossible concept to understand; the idea that a glob of matter could go through a man and not destroy him. There would most likely be some change and some effect, but there would not be a visible hole through him.

The universe is infinitely dense; what appears to be empty space is not. Just as the universe is infinitely dense, it is also infinitely empty. When we break a matchstick in half and discard half, cut it in half again and discard half, cut it in half and discard half, we will never arrive at a last piece, because even if there were a last piece, it would have to have dimension. And anything with dimension can be halved, assuming that we had the tools to do it, of course. You say we would get to a point where it would suddenly appear as energy? Energy has to be made up of something; it couldn't be nothing, unless you believed in magic. Any *stuff* can be cut in half, and cut in half, and cut in half again, which brings us to the realization that there is no final, tangible substance that we can take hold of in the universe. There is an infinity of nothing. Everything fades and disappears as we cut it. Let us restate that the universe is infinitely dense; since there is no such phenomenon as empty space and there is matter everywhere. But at the same time, matter has no substance. If we cut, and cut, and operated, and dissected, we would never arrive at the basic stuff of which material is made — it all fades into nothingness.

The universe is infinitely dense and does not exist.

12   A Catalog of Myths

The myths we believe in cause large organizations and our government to spend inordinate amounts of money on programs and policies which can get us nowhere. They cause confused and distressed individuals to look in the wrong direction for help. They cause our youth to be continually seduced and warped by irresponsible salesmen selling ideologies which are potentially destructive to our society. Because it has taken many years for these myths to develop and infiltrate, any attempt to lay them to rest would be feeble in the face of all that power. The immensity of the task can be appreciated when we realize that the myths abound in our writing, in our newspapers, in our cinema, in the content of our television programs, in our religions, in our therapeutic disciplines, and most seriously in our economics, political science, and in the design of our system.

This chapter is a catalog of myths: a compendium of unsane, scientifically invalid ideas, practices, beliefs, and opinions. Individuals do not easily give up their beliefs, even when exposed to their errors. Because of this, few will agree with all of the catalog, and more will object to the "truth" of the liberating tools presented to expose their favorite myths. To avoid involvement in a deep philosophic discussion concerning the nature of truth, we shall come to the point quickly by stating that the method used here to expose a fallacious idea is the method used by scientists in laboratory research.

It is the scientific method. It is not: "Will this apple fall to the ground if I release it?" but, "What is the probability of this apple falling to the ground if I release it?" Established fact, in science, means high probability.

Utilizing the scientific method, a scientist first performs experiments, or observes phenomena. Second, he forms a hypothesis to explain the phenomena, Third, he tests his hypothesis, since the scientific method is basically empirical, or cut and try. From these tests scientific laws are established, which are concerned only with the *how*, and not with the *why* (an unscientific word).

The scientific method is what has made possible all of our technology: our television, airplanes, rockets, and computers.

Scientists are rarely called upon to disprove a myth. The burden of proof, as in any argument on the existence of God, always lies with the claimant. But for the purpose of discussion, and in order to avoid a tedious explanation of how scientists hypothesize, test, and validate their hypotheses, we present the following example of a myth disproved:

Belief in Santa Claus is a myth.* How do we know, since there have been many sightings reported of a sleigh being pulled by reindeer through the Christmas sky? And what about those who still claim to have seen Santa climb down their chimneys? We know Santa Claus could not exist because:

> At the present state of the art, it is not aero-dynamically possible for all those reindeer to gallop through the sky.

*This example of a myth was written before the publication of Sagan's *The Cosmic Connection* which, by coincidence, uses the same Santa example. Since defeating the Santa myth is hardly original with anybody, we have decided to offer our version too. Apologies are extended to all disappointed children.

Santa couldn't cover, in one night, all the houses on his route, no matter how fast he flew.

Santa would have to have an immense sleigh to transport all the toys he delivers, a payload too large for a few reindeer to pull, requiring more horsepower than there are reindeer on earth.

Santa couldn't fit through most chimneys, especially the ones with fire screens installed.

He would be jet black from soot after his second or third visit, quite different from the white-bearded, red-faced, fur-lined and clean Santa with whom we are all familiar. All our gifts would be soot-stained, and they're not.

He would have to have millions of workers in his factory, and since it is located in the North Pole, he would be dependent on the delivery of an immense amount of raw material and supplies. The materials he requires do not exist at the North Pole, neither does the power. The entire world would be working in his factory or involved in supplying him with materials.

There are no mail deliveries to the North Pole, therefore all letters to Santa would go undelivered.

Since our letters would go undelivered, Santa could not know what each of us wanted for Christmas unless he had a vast intelligence organization involving millions of people who spent all year, from Christmas to Christmas, gathering information. And we know that one of us by now would have uncovered the plot.

And so forth.

Which demonstrates that we cannot trust the reports of sightings, or hearsay, or anecdotal evidence, not because people are intentionally untruthful, but because humans hallucinate and distort, distort in the sense that they stress what they want to believe and play down or forget any incidences which contradict their beliefs. For instance, many a mother has dreamed that her son away at war was killed in combat. Sometimes a mother receives a telegram the next morning announcing her son's death. We then easily forget about the thousands of times the dream didn't come true, but dramatize the once that it did, thus reinforcing a belief in the myth of clairvoyance, of some mysterious type of awareness.

People are not reliable observers, because they are neither equipped nor trained to observe. When we look with our eyes at the open palm of our hand we do not see germs, but when we look through a microscope we do. We are not *equipped* to see germs. When a ballerina and an engineer look at a modern jet aircraft engine they both see it, or do they? The engineer sees rotors and blades and igniters and ducts and controls and accessories in a functional relationship. What *does* the ballerina see? She is not technically trained to see an engine, therefore she sees nothing but a vague mass of metal. Only a structural engineer *sees* a bridge. How does a person without a motion picture production background look at a movie? To be sure he is affected by it, but a director sees it by observing camera angles, watching the actors, listening to the lines, listening to the music, checking the grain, contrast, and color of the film, checking the effect of scenes on the audience, noting the long, medium, and close-up shots, observing the dolly and truck shots, etc., etc. He sees so much more of the film than an untrained person.

To summarize, to believe in a myth, then, is to believe that something *is* when it *isn't* (Santa Claus) or to believe that something *isn't* when it *is* (germs). Also, to prove or disprove a myth we must use the *scientific method;* which means the use of telescopes, radar, microscopes, and cameras to verify, the use of laboratory test facilities to conduct empirical tests and measurement studies to check the aerodynamic possibilities of Santa flying through the air with all that payload, and to ascertain, with speed trials, whether he could visit all of those homes in the time allotted.

One might ask, "What is wrong with believing in a myth? Isn't ignorance sometimes bliss? When reality becomes painful, isn't it nice to know that one can escape into the fantasy of a myth?" To answer these questions we must examine the nature of *knowing.* What is the difference between individuals A and B when A "knows" aircraft engines and B doesn't? Is there a difference in their health, or performance, or efficiency, or in their behavior? The following should shed some light on the answer:

There is no evidence of a record in the brain; no master file of words, ideas, concepts, or pictures. Individuals are certainly affected by the environment in the sense that their behavior is changed by it. We do not know where or how in the organism this change takes place and how it occurs, but we do know that there is a change because of the change in behavior. One doesn't possess knowledge or know anything; one simply behaves differently. This is difficult to comprehend because of our habit of thinking about man as a thinking animal. We must turn our attention away from him, and toward the world around him, for an explanation of how and why he operates as he does. For now, let us remember that man does not behave spontaneously, and that his behavior is shaped by the external world, just as his genetic inheritance is shaped and selected by the world around him. So, in our example, we must realize that individual A has come under the control of external forces different from those of individual B, forces which make him more efficient and better able to cope with the world — of aircraft engines, at the least.

Some of the reasons why a belief in myths can be harmful are listed below:

> For society, the belief in a mythical social system such as free enterprise, which is based on a mythical law of supply and demand, creates a scarcity situation that breeds the kind of behavior known as crime, violence, war, disease, apathy, and the disorders noted in the next paragraph.

> For the individual, much time and energy is wasted going to "witch doctors" for treatment of behavioral disorders, based on the myth that the problem is inside some mythical mind when the solution lies in cleaning up the environment outside the individual. This myth seriously impedes recovery, may aggravate the condition, and in many cases results in serious damage to the individual and his family.

It is hoped that the following listing will arouse some interest in the methods of science and the scientific approach to the solution of our problems. Technology will inevitably change the world for the better, even though at the present it is creating adverse side affects. But only *more* technology can solve these side-effect problems; there is no turning back. Our choice is either the application of science to solve our problems, or a continued reliance on primitive myths.

Science versus chaos: only science and technology can save us. If not, what else will?

A Catalog of Myths

Myths	Liberating Tools
Astrology	Astronomy
Witchcraft	Medicine
Spirit, soul, animus	Biology, laboratory studies of the behavior of organisms
Sociology	Man-machine systems analysis, operations research
Custom, tradition, mores	Anthropology
Human nature	Genetics, laboratory research in learning behavior
Economics	A high-energy society, engineering control of resources, production, and distribution
Dollars, price, value based on scarcity	Value based on the required energy to produce products in an abundant society
Law of supply and demand	Regulation, load factor control

Myths	*Liberating Tools*
Humanistic psychology, demon possession, exorcism, witchcraft, UFO's, reincarnation, ESP, est, occultism, scientology, telekinesis, levitation, faith healing, primal or secondary screaming, phILOSophy	Engineering studies of the machine that is man
Ignorance, bias, dogma, prejudice, racism, crime, poverty	Equal access to learning. The technological operation of society, each citizen assured of an abundance of goods and services
False language; words such as *truth, beauty, life, intelligence, motivation, will*	Tentative statements of probability, mathematics, accuracy and clarity of statement based on laboratory observation and measurement
Beginning, end	Infinity, space-time continuum
Man as something special and apart, ethnocentrism	Man as part of the universe
Earth as center of world	Copernicus, Galileo
Man as a unique and superior species	Darwin, Wallace, DeVries

Myths	*Liberating Tools*
Newton, classical physics	Einstein, relativity
Communication of ideas between humans	Verbal behavior
Knowing, awareness, intelligence	Conditioning, the study of survival behavior as genetic inheritance
Thinking	Subvocalization, covert behavior
Ignorance is bliss. We lose something when we become aware	Knowledge is power; knowing is efficient, healthful behavior
Idea that other planets in universe must have technologically advanced civilizations ready to communicate with us	Elimination of TRAP thinking through new definitions of terminology and concepts; avoidance of anthropomorphism
Study of man as a human	A realization that to look at man as other than a machine is to waste time and effort
Laissez-faire, anarchy, free enterprise, competition	Freedom through control; stopping at a traffic light assures freedom of safety and the right to live
Affluence, celebrity, power	The application of engineering and science to

184 IS THERE INTELLIGENT LIFE ON EARTH?

Myths	*Liberating Tools*
	the solution of social problems guarantees affluence for all; awareness that affluence, celebrity, and power are today realized at the expense of others
Architecture; the artistic expression of the architect in the design of dwellings	Replacement of architecture as an art-form by the design and mass production of maximum shelters with optimum materials; the automobile production concept applied to homes; houses designed to be machines for healthful living, rather than kitsch-traditional-handcrafted-hammer-and-nailed wood boxes
Automobiles; a high horse-power engine for each citizen	Circular cities designed with mass transportation systems for efficient, healthful, and faster people-moving
Ownership	Availability of products and services for use only when needed; concept that a product has no value unless used; realization

Myths	*Liberating Tools*
	that ownership today means simply proximity and availability
Mother instinct	Skilled specialists in child training; the nursery school idea expanded to its logical conclusion
Freedom to bear children	Population control
Freedom to exploit children through the mythical escapism, fantasyland, and violence of television, books, and motion pictures	Child-rearing centers that train children early to be scientifically and socially aware; elimination of advertising in a technically operated society
The virtue of work	Agreement that if man liked to work he wouldn't have invented machines; dehumanizing human labor (1/6 HP per day) replaced by other more efficient sources of energy and automated production; contribution of approximately 5 hrs/week maximum involvement contributed by all citizens up to age of 35, in addition to guaranteed education for lifetime

Myths	*Liberating Tools*
Business, law, finance, advertising, sales, investment banking	A social system operated by scientists and engineers dedicated to the production and distribution of all the goods and services needed for a long, healthful life; the elimination of vague hypotheses such as economics and other non-technical approaches
Privately endowed science research programs; company sponsored research	Socially oriented research
Male supremacy	Application of the idea that acculturally-reinforced sexual stereo-typing cannot survive when the economic dependence of one human on another is eliminated and all have equal access to education
Sensationalism, titillation, slanderous gossip, and incitement to violence masquerading as news in the popular press and television	News re-defined as socially significant events

Myths	*Liberating Tools*
Charisma, personality, and public relations determining who is elected to public office	Competence and ability as criteria; the pilot of an airliner is not elected by a popular vote of the passengers but is in command because of his ability to operate the aircraft safely
Religion, pie-in-the-sky-when-you-die, superstition, ignorance	Anthropology, genetics, biology, physics, chemistry, behavioral technology
Psychoanalysis; gestalt; humanistic psychology; bio-energetics; primal, secondary, or tertiary screaming	Behavior as an applied science; laboratory studies of the behavior of organisms, environmental control and manipulation
Man's natural life expectancy	Prolongation of life through micro-cellular studies of genetics and the gerontological effects of aging; use of prosthetics and artificial organs to extend man's life indefinitely
Da-daism, cubism, impressionism, brush squeezing, surrealism	Color and design used to enhance man's environment; graphics, perspective, anatomy, rendering, the science of drawing, projective

Myths	*Liberating Tools*
	geometry, projection of objects on a flat plane, considered essential for training of young people to assure structurally – honest observation of reality
Heterosexuality as normal behavior. Other sexual preferences considered deviant. Homosexuality as illness.	Recognition that sexual preferences are acculturally conditioned and not natural or normal; no law, morality, or value judgements applied to adult behavior.
Intelligence, IQ testing, "superior" and "inferior" used to rate and grade individual's behavior.	Kinship with all humanity, warmth and acceptance of all organisms anywhere on the planet.
Computers utilized to increase profits; systems sold to consumers for the purpose of playing war games.	Utilization of computer technology and machine intelligence to manage and monitor production and distribution of products.
Elementary schools, high schools, college.	Children's centers to raise healthy, socially aware and responsible citizens; the aim of learning not the attainment of a profession or a skill but awareness of the inter-relationships of

Myths	*Liberating Tools*
	the environment to organisms; students trained to think in terms of the overall pattern of life, rather than sheer gratification and the extension of comfort.
Future will bring tall buildings, superhighways and humanity marching around in translucent clothing like automatons.	Planned circular cities, dotted with green forests, parks and lakes, with maximum comfort and security provided for everyone.
Production for profit with men working for a subsistence wage to make other men rich; slavery; noblesse oblige.	Quiet production centers with automation fully utilized; billions of voice-actuated electronic slaves to serve man.
Energy sources limited by the reserves of our planet.	Solar energy; energy tapped from the Van Allen belt of radiation that surrounds the earth; nuclear energy free of pollution and unsafe radiation effects.
Medical diagnosis limited to physician's skills and experience.	Advanced scanning devices to sweep anatomy and select the most appropriate treatment for specific problems within micro-seconds.

Myths	*Liberating Tools*
Success of surgery limited to surgeon's skills and experience.	Programmed surgery performed almost automatically.
Fault, no-fault, blame, credit, bravery, cowardliness, right, wrong.	The concept of culpability discarded; no-fault society based on the premise that individuals are not to be blamed or credited for their behavior since all organisms are under the control of the environment.
Self-esteem, self-reliance, independence, self-sufficiency.	Family extended to its ultimate concept; people need people.
Competition, teamwork, football, baseball.	Competition between individuals and groups considered harmful and destructive; socially aware and responsible people do not compete in a secure society.
Philosophy, speculation, personal opinion.	Observation, experiment; science, the scientific method; decision-making by machines, computers, and instrumentation.
Pre-nursery school, nursery school, kindergarten, elementary school.	Education beginning in the womb.

Myths	*Liberating Tools*
Non-productive years, retirement, rest.	Continued participation in the activities of society; non-productive years not recognized; care of physical disabilities guaranteed.
Creative freedom in schools, unstructured environment, self-expression.	Accelerated learning through a structured environment; since we are all under the control of *some* environment, a planned, designed, structured environment is no more structured than a so-called free environment; children provided with optimal training through ordered environment.
Computers, calculating machines, analytic engines.	World sensors, capable of sensing all phenomena necessary in the management of human affairs, far beyond the collective intelligence of all people.
The personal worth of students measured by school grades.	Noncompetitive education stressing cooperation and teamwork; shaping and learning through control of in-vitro and in-vivo experience.

Myths	*Liberating Tools*
Airplanes dependent on forward speed for safety.	Anti-gravity propulsion systems generating G forces.
Verbal communication, the communication of ideas between humans.	Verbal communication as verbal behavior, studies of social and cultural differences; value modification; learning how to state a problem solves verbal inadequacies.
There are limits to human perception.	Human perception continually exceeding limits through the electron microscope, time compression, and analytic instrumentation able to translate billions of events in nanoseconds.
There are limits to man's growth.	Man's growth continually generates the next stage of human evolution, from man to androids to cybernated organisms, which in turn generate a still higher form of integration capable of modifying its own forms until it merges with the space-time continuum.

13   Welcome to Tomorrow

Science is made up of technical men, who are generally industrious and peaceful. Without science, the executive limousines would cease to move, and the offices of the President would be uninhabitable. The only qualifications needed for a leader of the United States is charisma, personality, and perhaps an ability to "tell the Russians off". The qualifications of a director in a society managed by technologists would be the ability to operate a complex mechanism consuming millions of kilowatts of energy. Imagine for a moment a Nixon, a Kennedy, or a Carter in charge of a complex functional mechanism that has to be operated, not merely charmed.

Corporation heads know very little about the technical aspects of the enterprises they head. They are not as concerned with turning out useful and durable products as they are with sales and profits. This is where the advertising business comes in — to convince the consumer to buy one company's product over another. Also to buy two products instead of one; two cars, two telephones, two bathrooms, two wigs. Instead of stereo, now it's four speakers, and soon four wigs.

Television is exposing these people. When one watches a political convention in the United States it is hard not to notice the nonsense that goes on, since television exposes and dramatizes all the silliness in a very obvious manner. If meetings of Congress were televised, they would soon reveal their foolishness to the American public. As in the case of practicing attorneys, as long as there is an illusion of mystery they can continue to operate.

Dramatic changes in our culture are now taking place. Mass production on a continental scale will inevitably be developed and transportation systems will be designed to accomodate shifts in urban centers. The highest priority will be assigned to scientific research and its technological applications. *Computers and engineering systems will have a greater effect within the next 25 years than all of the political bickering of the world's past history.* The world of today, with its archaic language systems and vague economic practices, is already on its way out, and as the demand for science continues to accelerate, it will bypass and leave behind all cultures and individuals unable to grasp its significance.

What we of today think of life in the future is irrelevant; the future will be for a new person. There is no way for us to evaluate, within the bounds of our present value system, what living in the future will be like. Already the money system is proving, by its inequities and its maldistribution of wealth, that it doesn't work.

The Money System On Its Way Out

The dollar led to the check system, and check writing is almost universal today. The check system will be replaced by the charge card, which has become a computerized way of purchasing goods and services. And now we have salaries deposited directly to our bank accounts, so there is no need for a transfer of funds from pocket to pocket. Soon it will become evident to us that the waste of energy involved in managing the transfer the money from organism to organism is unproductive and totally inefficient.

In the near future, it really won't matter what a person's worth is, all people will posses unlimited credit. A system such as that would be much cheaper and easier to maintain than the system we have today. Banks with their clerks, the entire finance industry, the need to oversee and monitor accounts and hold individuals accountable and responsible for finances are already obsolete; it is much easier to disregard a person's financial state and simply allow him to charge limitlessly. To conceive of that with our present value system is almost impossible, but with today's technological techniques, products have become so inexpensive to produce that there is an overabundance of them, and it behooves us to stimulate demand by distributing them free rather than by reducing the price; the ultimate price reduction is simply to give it away. Today we need not have enough money in our checking accounts to cover all our check writing activities because of the ready reserve system that many banks are utilizing; this is the system that permits the bank to deposit money to your account even when you are short, to assure you that there will never be a lack of cash for your check-writing activities.

Well, then, where does it stop? Why shouldn't it take its next step, which is to allow an infinite reserve for all peoples? This is being done even without a redesign of society and our social affairs.

When it comes, yes, we will assure the distribution of an abundance to all, but we will not assure the proper design of our country for maximum efficiency. If automation and advanced technological production techniques were fully exploited and our machines were allowed to run on a 24-hour basis rather than simply 8 hours and turned off for 16 as they are today (a balanced load of production), our largest problem would be the distribution of these goods. Uninhibited production is not the answer; planning must be based on consumption capacity, and projections must be made for the next period's needs.

The money system, which assigns value and price to a product, is already obsolete. Value today is based on scarcity, the harder to get the more expensive. If it's available, price goes down. This is false value based on archaic economic concepts. Product value in the future will be based on the energy required to produce that product. People will be assigned a sufficient quantity of purchasing power to satisfy more than their needs for a stipulated period, based on a computerized analysis of the nation's needs of the last period and the available resources. Products will be optimally designed; there will be no designing for obsolescence since sales and profit are not the objective. Vehicles will be designed to last and run, and the concept of the individual automobile, with its pollution and traffic problems, will be phased out.

The idea of ownership is already being replaced by the leasing and rental systems. Products are dispensable and are only valuable when used. A thing has no value when it is hanging in the closet or sitting in the garage. Today ownership means proximity — if you own a Cadillac it means that you have access to it.

Ownership never means that you can ingest the product except in the case of food. Products never become part of us, so the word *ownership* is misleading. Accessibility is the key word. If motor cars were instantly available at the end of our telephone, this is all that we would require; it is the leasing system extended to its maximum. But of course the concept will not mean an individual motor car for each organism, but mass transit. Mass transit by today's standards does not appear attractive; but it will be a more efficient, more comfortable, less nerve-wracking, healthier, and safer way to move masses of humanity than the present one-man-per-ton-of-metal jammed on the freeways and throughways throughout the nation, consuming energy and polluting the atmosphere at a high and intolerable rate.

With an engineering and technological design of our social system we can immediately avail ourselves of computer technology. Today computers are utilized mainly to increase profits; brightly packaged systems are sold to consumers to play games of war and other games of nonsensical competition. The ideal utilization of computer technology would be in the adaptation of it to machine intelligence and creativity. Computers will manage undersea farms, and volcanic and tidal power. Technology will govern and control children's centers where young and healthy people, socially aware and responsible, will be raised. Future lifestyles will be affected, and a human existence which we never before have imagined is in store for us in the near tomorrow.

It is difficult for us to set aside our prejudices and accept all of this without qualm. We prefer the idea of people working as individuals — competing, achieving success or failure, and formulating decisions on their own to face any consequences when they're wrong. The argument goes that freedom from stress is not desirable and would not be worth the cost to our individuality. The fact that it will end individual differences appears to be a threat to today's person. Our greatest fear is the unfamiliar, but that is today's thinking applied to tomorrow's person.

The Future —
Reality vs Science Fiction

How would you like to explore the world whenever you felt like it? To attend schools or not? To reliably depend for your safety and security on socially integrated computers? If you would, then welcome to tomorrow. It will not be like the trekkies and star warriors depict, with tall buildings, superhighways, and people walking around in translucent clothing. It will be more human than today, with forests, warm fragrances, and maximum comfort and security provided for everyone. Cities will be mostly parks, with ferns and flowers and dense greenery. The landscape will be dotted with lakes where one will observe boats moving silently through the waters.

The aim of all learning will not be the attainment of a profession, a skill, or a specialty, but a deep awareness of the interrelationships of the environment to organisms in the space-time continuum. Because of our genetic endowment we will recognize even more that touching, being held, and played with are very important components in the development of children. Concepts like anger and hurt will not even be remotely understood by tomorrow's children, who will be trained to think in terms of the overall pattern of life rather than self-centered gratification and comfort.

Imagine being accepted anywhere you went without feeling a sense of being alone — a fellowship with all people, a warmth and an acceptance by all, anywhere on the surface of this planet. This is *family*. Behavioral science (of a kind we cannot begin to imagine today because it will use technological aids of all sorts) will be utilized extensively. Human systems will be looked upon as capable of many changes, and there is no doubt that future people will exceed the limits of time and space.

In the production centers we will not hear any noise, but a faint hum. There will be no displays of information, readouts, knobs, dials, and levers since automation will be fully utilized in a technologically designed society. Think of machines as millions if not billions of electronic slaves, and that's what we will have at our disposal. Electronic circuitry will be sub-microscopic. Aircraft will no longer be based on lift systems but on electrostatically-polarized propulsion systems, cancelling out or neutralizing the gravitational pull of the earth. Advanced metallurgical techniques (if we wish to call it metallurgy) will lead to the control of molecular locks, which means that we will molecularly lock even incompatible materials together so that the union of materials will be seam-free. There will be transparent steel everywhere, material as strong and as transparent as glass. Solar energy will be our primary source of power, and nuclear energy will be free of pollution and unsafe radiation effects.

Vast production centers, silent and unmanned by humans, will produce enclosure systems (presently known as homes), transportation units, and other products. The age of wheels will be long past; linear induction trains will move us from point to point. And all electronic slaves will be voice actuated, obeying our every wish and command.

Information systems will be stored on a molecular level, as opposed to today's magnetic tapes and charged core systems. In medicine, advanced scanning devices will optically sweep our anatomy and select the most appropriate surgery for specific problems within microseconds. The internal structures of bacteria will be manipulated by microscanning techniques. The problem of aging will be overcome, and in the near future, life expectancies will certainly be beyond 300 years, and eventually immortality.

New techniques will arise in the field of fetal surgery, where defects will be detected and corrected before birth. Advances will be made in the neuro-surgical control of pain with nerve-grafting techniques. Cutting and coagulating currents will divide tissue and seal vessels of blood. Prosthetics, artificial organs, and artificial eyes and ears will be part of this new and exciting world. Computers programmed to behave as humans will demonstrate the meaning of *intelligent life.** Surgery will be performed almost entirely automatically; how many lives will be preserved when the factors of human error and malpractice are eliminated cannot be calculated today.

*If only today's phILOSophers could be there.

In the area of interpersonal relationships we must remember that, today, in order to consult with another human being, we have to talk or touch in order to communicate or share values. There are hazy semantic blockages and problems generated because of this technique. In the future, linguistics will not be as important as an awareness of a new approach to *value modification*, a concept which cannot be explained or understood with today's language. It is as difficult for us to escape our conditioning as it would be for the future humans to adopt such concepts as "deceit" and "personal politics". Such traits as anger, guile, revenge, and hatred will have no meaning in the future, whose people will be as alien to our physical and behavioral makeup as we are to a flea.

We cannot make a start in this direction until the money system collapses. It will collapse — it is inevitable. The day of shoddy goods, junk, poverty, and all of its attendant problems is rapidly coming to a close, as our politicians waddle about aimlessly, frantically grabbing all they can in the hysterical process of trying to maintain themselves politically and physically.

We are all on the edge of extinction no matter how rich we think we are. If we are poor, we have to work for a living and worry about emergency medical bills. Even millionaires are poor because we are all, millionaire and pauper alike, living under the threat of the bomb. We are all staring at the same meaningless torpor of television, and involved in the fantasyland of movies. We are all conditioned to think alike; our value systems are made uniform and distorted by the barrage of media that surrounds and absorbs us. Overpopulation at an unbridled pace is killing us all. The poor are increasing astronomically. The rich are intensifying their richness and concentrating it into the hands of fewer and fewer. Technological unemployment is a reality and will increase at a high rate of speed. Our problems present the ultimate challenge for systems engineers and operations research types; what production engineers are doing inside factories today will be done on a national scale.

The Selling Out of American Science

There are few things worse than the sight of a myopic scientist who is unconcerned or unaware of what his fellow humans are doing, because he is not living in the real world. There is one thing worse, and that is a scientist who will deliberately exploit people by popularizing his science, and cater to the morbid interest of those who are addicted to flying saucer and science fiction myths. There is money today in "popular" science. There is also money in show business science, in the kind that appears occasionally on "educational" television under the guise of a history of science, whose perpetrators are more interested in building a saleable image of themselves than sharing a truth and uplifting their fellow man.

There is a chapter in one of the phILOSopher's books entitled *What Do You Say to a Non-Human?* In the book entitled *The Cosmic Connection,* by another phILOSopher, the message riding on board *Pioneer 10* is described, the 6 x 9 inch gold-anodized aluminum plate designed to tell the story of we marooned organisms on Earth to alien civilizations that might intercept the spacecraft. There is a book entitled *Is Anyone Out There?* written by two phILOSophers, another one called *We Are Not Alone,* still another one entitled *Is Anyone There?* and many more to come.

What we should be asking is, "What Do You Say to a *Human? What* we should be concerned with is not mythical people in the Cosmos but *Humanity-on-Earth.* 6 x 9 messages scrawled on plaques should be sent to every citizen of the United States welcoming him to the *community of man*. Is anyone out there? Maybe. But there are certainly plenty here to be worried about. Writers and movie makers have the creative right to speculate on any science subject they will, but let's call it what it is, science *fiction* and not science. And let's label the objectives for what they are, exploitation and sales rather than education. Whether or not they succeed in contacting "aliens", they are certainly communicating very profitably with Earthlings.

The phILOSophers are the products of the social instability of our times and their numbers will increase until that social instability exceeds the limits of tolerance; then our society will have to be staffed by socially-conscious scientists who are competent to meet the needs of our citizens. PhILOSophers are forced to exploit because our whole economy is based on an archaic method of valuation. Money, which is archaic, must give way to the quantitative methods of physical science applied to the evaluation of products and services. All scientists, engineers, technologists, and technical people should be aware of the importance of a self-contained functional system, for they will soon be called upon to operate it. This, and only this, will guarantee a high standard of living with equality of income and maximum security at a minimum of working hours for everyone.

Lest the reader dismiss this as the ravings of a frothing-at-the mouth revolutionary, be advised that what we are recommending is not a political party and has nothing in common with any other social or utopian system. What we are recommending is that American scientists and technologists become aware of their importance and power, and be ready to operate our society when chaos comes, as it will when our money system collapses.

Then, welcome to tomorrow.

What Will Happen
14   To Our Cities?

We are forced to ask: about this wonderful world that will
be technologically directed in a functional manner to
provide maximum comfort and security for all people, how
is it supposed to happen? If it happens suddenly, what will
happen to our existing world? Think of New York City, an
undesigned city that grew like Topsy, here and there, without planning. What will we do? Will we raze the skyscrapers, tear down the bridges, burn the slums, run
bulldozers through the whole city, flatten it, demolish it, so
that we can build over again?

What will happen to the theaters, the movie palaces, the
vast underground network of sewers, utility systems, and
subways under the city? The transportation systems, the
automobiles, the people? How will this wonderful world of
tomorrow begin? Will everything come to a screeching halt
and then suddenly start anew?

When we read the daily newspapers it is hard to believe
that the ideas expressed in this book will ever come about.
There are kings and queens and politicians, there are rich
men, celebrities, actors, actresses, all behaving as if chaos
were not around the corner. It is easy to be carried away by
the force of all that exists today, by the conditioning that the
media overlays on each individual as he reads the news and
views it on television. It is hard to believe that the material
in this book could possibly be true, could be other than
visionary, utopian, or idealistic.

The breakdown, the chaos to which we vaguely refer throughout the book will come about through crises such as a sudden shortage and failure of the sources of energy: light, power, and heat. Another source of crisis will be inflation, which will soar to such a high rate that products will be priced out of the market, far outstripping any gains in wages and salaries achieved by the customer.

Another source of crisis will be toxic and chemical, in the form of pollution, dirt, uncontrolled and runaway poisons in the atmosphere, in our foods, in our water supply, and in our agriculture. Another will be the vast military machine armed so heavily and poised with weaponry enough to destroy the world 100 times over, itching to be utilized. And all of these crises will probably occur in roughly the same time period.

Another crisis will be the crisis in transportation, with traffic snarls that will increase to the point where mobility is reduced to zero. This will probably happen shortly in most of the big cities of the United States. And as a result, there will be food shortages which will lead to riot and panic conditions.

It is easy to look the other way, as we do every day, and ignore what we are saying. All seems well when we read the newspapers, view and listen to the news, or involve ourselves in the fantasyland of television and motion picture entertainment. *But the reality is that the crisis is here; we are in the middle of it, and too far into it to understand that it is here, because there is no way for us to observe it.*

Another major source of crisis will be the emotional effect on humans expressed in an increase in irritability and tension, in dependence on drugs, in murder and violence, as a result of the collapsing economic system and the accompanying propaganda to acquire more and more.

When the riots and the chaos come, how is this wonderful utopian world of tomorrow to come into being? It could go either way. There could be a dictatorship imposed by a military clique who would take over the reins and enforce a so-called peace on the community. But, if it is to last, it has to be controlled by scientists and engineers; that is why a scientific society is inevitable unless we are wiped out by a nuclear bomb.

There are those among us who are aware of the crisis and are preparing for it, hoping that it won't touch them, but we will all be touched by the chaos. Some are hungrily reading "survival" literature, buying weapons to "protect themselves", and stocking up on emergency rations, preparing for the death of society.

And there are the terrorists who feel that overthrowing the system could lead to something better. Little do they realize that we have the most obvious solution to our problems, the most advanced technological operation on earth, ready and willing to serve us.

We also have the religionists and cultists who are expecting supernatural intervention or hoping that there will be pie-in-the-sky-when-we-die. And we musn't forget the gophers who would have us dig our way underground to carry on the money system as usual in the event of a nuclear holocaust. Although their solution is unsane, the fact remains that in a money system a nuclear war is a real possibility and, frighteningly, the decision for that happening lies in the hands of the fools who have the power.

But the paradox remains, that our scientists and technologists are unaware of their power to solve our problems. Years ago, we could dust off the family rifle and dash into the streets to protect our families in time of trouble, but our problems today require the skills that only our engineers can provide. We can only hope they will wake up.

Rising from the Ashes

After the collapse of the money system, we will rebuild. But instead of rebuilding the old, new cities will be started where no cities were before. Planning will involve transportation systems and the development of giant production and distribution centers to care for the population. At first, life will be spartan with no place for style, color, and luxury. Clothing, transportation systems, and shelter will be functional, serving no need but to meet the emergency. But as technological planning develops from year to year, the new society will evolve.

The advantage that we have in the United States is that we have the technological know-how, the facilities, and the resources to achieve the new society almost overnight; that is the one optimistic note in the entire picture. It can be done today, and if we could avoid the chaos, it could be a painless transition. But those in power — those who have the money, the politicians, businessmen, and the lawyers — are not about to give up what they have. Revolution is not the answer. All we can do is to understand the nature of technical operations and grow with the scientific age, because those who do not understand science and technical planning will be left by the wayside, as the new age approaches and surpasses them.

As an emergency measure, the very first action taken will be to restore the energy sources so that productive power can be placed into action again; high production will be necessary to ensure an adequate food supply to the populace, since the availability of food will depend on production and agriculture, which in turn will depend on technology, which will depend on energy sources to function.

Society today is operated by technical people but they are not in command. They are the ones who are responsible for the factories working, the transportation operating, and the utilities functioning. Because they are not at the helm there is no planning of these functions. But the source of this skill and knowledge is here, still operating the same mechanism. The major source of disturbance will be in their assumption of the planning and control function which they have never had in the past, and it will be accompanied by delay and many trials until they have solved for the most functional approach. The problem is one of industrial engineering, the operation of the United States being no different than the internal operation of a factory, and if it is operated the way industrial engineers and planners utilize in the operation of a factory it will work.

Of course resistance is to be expected. There are many unsane philosophies, cults, concepts, religions, superstitions, and power groups with imagined self-interest that will buck and resist any new society, but they will fall by the wayside as they are supplied with an ever-abundant flow of goods to satisfy their needs. As children are better educated and grow up in a more healthful manner, the resistance to child-raising centers will subside dramatically. The freedom of people from humdrum, dehumanizing work will mark the beginning of a liberation for all those who are suppressed today: women, minorities, the deprived, the slow and the retarded, those with unpopular sexual preferences, the aged, and the young. It will also mark the beginning of the no-fault society, whose trends are seen even today, and the advent of automation, liberating most people from work. Education, adventure, and travel will be pursued evermore with less and less time demands made on individuals. Timekeeping devices such as calendars and clocks will fade away since there will be no need to know the time of the day, the day of the month, or even the year, although they will continue to be utilized in scientific research. Not caring about what day of the month it is, or even what year, will be one of the major tension-relievers in the history of man.

There is no doubt that the transition will be painful fo⁻

many, but the pain will only occur in the transition, and then subside to a point far below where it is today. There will be less emotional problems and more security, with crime almost reduced to zero and poverty eliminated. And once we pass through the birth pangs we will begin a life such as we cannot envision by today's standards or describe by today's language.

What will happen to today's educated men who no longer will have a niche in tomorrow: businessmen, salesmen, lawyers, accountants, financiers of all sorts, anybody whose work is related to the business of selling and the money system? The same thing that will happen to the rest of us — we will all be expected to participate in tasks outside our professions, our work hours reducing gradually as automation takes over.

What will happen to the artists, the poets, the painters, the composers, the jazz musicians, entertainers, actors, mimes, ballet dancers, playwrights, producers, journalists, publishers, and sculptors? They will continue their work on a grander scale, but there is no doubt that the education of the young will change tomorrow's attitude toward the art, entertainment, and poetry of today.

Yes, we will be faced with countless problems during the transition phase. Think of the people who are emotionally disturbed: the anxious people, the depressed people, the slow people, the hostile people, the terminally ill people, the undersexed people, the oversexed people, the child batterers, the children of broken homes, and the others.

Food, clothing, shelter, and freedom from stress may not provide the answers they require. But abundance and freedom from poverty will bring us more than a fresh start; it will be the dream of centuries come true, a historic event that will transcend anything ever before accomplished by man. If applied science will not work, what will?

15   10 Do's and 10 Do Not's

What subjects should a person study to prepare for the new society? With what background should he provide himself so that his skills could be utilized effectively? The following ten suggestions are offered:

1. **Investigate** the critically important material produced by our behavioral scientists. Especially check the research done by B.F. Skinner, a contemporary colossus years ahead of his time.

2. **Examine** the clear and forcibly written literature published by Technocracy, Inc. This excellent organization, which has been around since the 30s, is small and powerless, but nevertheless still provides us with a rich source of data related to the collapse of the money system. Technocracy (spelled with a capital T) was first theorized by Thorstein Veblen, then carried out by Howard Scott, with the help of GE's wizard Steinmetz. The organization is made up of scientists, engineers, and lay people who are keenly aware of the social implications of science and technology.

3. **Study** production methods and techniques. Inquire into the nature of synthetic materials, metallurgy, forming and stamping techniques, machine shop practice, computerized and automated factories. It is all very relevant to our social problems.

4. **Search** the literature for work done in city planning and design, urban planning, air quality control, and communities designed for people. There has never been a planned city in the history of our planet, but public interest in the field is increasing daily as the citizens of our decaying cities become more concerned with the future quality of their lives.

5. **Question** everything published in the West about how the Soviet Union and Chinese People's Republic work. While their systems are based on money, not technologically controlled, and not adaptable to our high energy society, it is important that we learn to be unbiased, open-minded, and aware of how other systems operate.

6. **Probe** into the technical nature of computers and micro-processors. Find out what they are about, as they will become socially important once we stop playing silly games with them. Like television, they are a perfect example of a technology presently utilized in socially harmful ways.

7. **Reflect** on the works of anthropologists, whose concern is the evolution and behavior of groups of people and cultures; their customs, mores, lifestyles, and religions. Expose your children to this subject in their early, formative years.

8. **Inquire** into the teachings of Charles Darwin. Immerse youself in the study of your relationship to all other life forms on this planet. Learn how we originated, how we developed, how the selection process works, and about the process of mutations.

9. **Meditate,** during quiet evening hours alone, with books on astronomy, cosmology, and physics, until you become intensely aware of the place of our unimportant, yet important, planet in this dark, mysterious universe. Study the many popular translations of Einsteinian relativity written for the non-scientist; they will give you a sweeping and comprehensive view of the nature of the world, and leave you forever changed as a person.

10. **Contemplate** the staggeringly realistic views of the future published by Jacque Fresco, the founder of Sociocyberneering. There are many futurists, "geniuses", and self-styled seers in our midst who, upon careful examination, turn out to be disappointingly commercial and exploitive. Most extrapolations into the future are made from fixed and narrow points of view (see Chapter 1, TRAP 1). We are all products of today's mediocrity-breeding culture, but if anyone can be called a genius in our money system society, Jacque Fresco should be singled out as the broadest, most aware, individual of our time.

The following are ten things *not* to do:

1. **Do not** study history. There is little value in names, dates, and places. Historic trends and events in our low-energy past have little relationship to the present high-energy problems of our technologically advanced society. Engineers, city planners, and computer specialists do not look back to the 19th century for answers.

2. **Do not** become entangled with the occult, est, esp, astrology, humanistic psychology — from psychoanalysis through primal screaming, flying saucers,

colonic irrigation, aliens from outer space, science fiction, the flat earth society, dolphin intelligence, the Turin shroud, UFOs, holy rollers, churches and temples of any denomination, charms and miraculous cures, Hollywood movies, exorcism, ghosts, clairvoyance, levitation, chariots of the gods, economics — both Keynesian and Friedmanian, pet rocks, television, star trekkies, star warriors, encounterers of the third kind, the ballot box, phILOSophy, or geodesic domes.

3. **Do not** worship at the Altar of the Dollar. Don't be ambitious or ruthless in your work. If you must step on others to maintain or advance your position, or if your product or service is socially harmful, look for another job. Go on welfare if necessary; it will hasten the demise of the money system.

4. **Do not** listen to, or read, the news unless it has some significance to your life. Most published news is gossip and most television news is entertainment. The roof rescue of a stranded cat is not news; stories of the comings and goings of Hollywood celebrities are not news. Murders are not news. Develop an interest in what is happening on a national or international scale that will affect the survival of our species.

5. **Do not** succumb to trends, fashions, fads, or styles; in your clothing, in your car, in your values, in your lifestyle, in your eating habits, in your furnishings, or in your home. These are foisted upon you by cynical sales and advertising people to stimulate business. Look for utility and function in the products that you buy and the values that you espouse. Don't be dupable, deludable, or hoodwinkable; don't be an easy prey to the hucksters or salesmen of the money system,

whether they are trying to sell you clothing, religion, facelifts, anti-communism, or war.

6. **Do not** patronize lawyers or become involved in the law if you can possibly avoid it. The adversary system of law is based on a doctrine of contentious procedure, an archaic leftover of primitive times, whose object is winning, not justice. Unless he is working in the public interest, a lawyer's first loyalty, after his pocketbook, is to his client, which places many obstacles in the path of truth. Most lawyers, to be successful, are forced by the money system to be unscrupulous. They are prime examples of a people degraded by the system, a system which, in law especially, reinforces our most destructive ethic.

7. **Do not** deal with the advertising business or its peddlers, unless you have a socially important message to proclaim. The central ethic of the advertising game is "Don't worry whether it's true or not. Sell it." Advertising is mostly falsehood, deception, mendacity, mystification, distortion, fraud, evasion, sham, duplicity, untruth, hypocrisy, humbug, perfidy, artfulness, double-dealing, misrepresentation, prevarication, equivocation, exaggeration, and bull.

8. **Do not** think of criminals as criminal. Do not find fault with anybody. The principle of culpability is dead. Think of a faultless society. Remember that nobody is to blame for anything because we are all products of our culture, including lawyers, advertising people, and salesmen. This is the scientific version of the Christian ethic "Forgive them for they know not what they do."

9. **Do not** attend any house of worship or religious temple, unless you wish to socialize. "Holiness" is not the luxury of a few clergy. It is a simple duty for each of us, and through *applied love* we can become holy. If God does exist, he would want you to study science and engineering so that you could act out your love for your fellow man, whatever his color or shape, by providing him with an abundant, long, and fruitful life through the mastery of his problems.

10. **Do not** resolve to take charge of your life, assert yourself, do your own thing, or look out for Number 1. The charlatans who believe that each individual is an autonomous island steering itself through life are the same people who still believe in the Easter Bunny. Most of the "how to better yourself" books that are presently selling like hotcakes are psychologically invalid. We are all dependent on each other; for our survival, for our welfare, and for our happiness. People need people. This is the scientific version of the Christian credo "Love your fellow person".

Epilogue

Total cities have to be designed in America, not by architects expressing their creativity on a building-by-building basis, but by city planners skilled in the design of man-machine systems. There will be color and beauty in the city, with heavy emphasis placed on human environmental needs such as forests and wooded areas. A stroll through the city of tomorrow would take us through flora and parks where children will be seen playing. We would see cultural centers featuring large areas devoted to the arts and music, with people attending these attractions without payment or tickets of any kind. What would be startling to a person of today would be the sparse population and the strange silence over the city.

Since the planned cities of tomorrow will be radial, there will be radial conveyors to move people to and from the central core to the outer ring, and circular conveyors to transport them around each ring. As the radial conveyors carry a person outward, he would pass over crystal clear lakes and streams, and through forests of flowers and dark greenery.

There will be children's centers for advanced training, highly structured environments adjusted to the developmental rate of each child. The new technology would startle today's person. Giant production centers, operated by a social integrator, will silently form and shape all the products required for human needs. Voice-actuated devices of all sorts will act as electronic slaves for all citizens. The new leisure will allow people to spend most of their time in education, travel, and adventure.

Symposiums on world affairs will be held at vast domed centers designed to house super-intelligent computers with three-dimensional displays. These control centers will be capable of making optimum decisions on billions of simultaneous events in nanoseconds. They will transcend and exceed the limits of human physiological systems by such a magnitude that they will be capable of accurately extrapolating present events to many years ahead.

Time has no respect for individuals or cultures. The bio-social forces that shape the future are lawful. The future, like the present, is the result of the primary forces of the space-time continuum.

It is happening. It is important that we be ready for it.

Index